THE

Psychic Workbook

Tools and Techniques
to Develop Reliable Insight

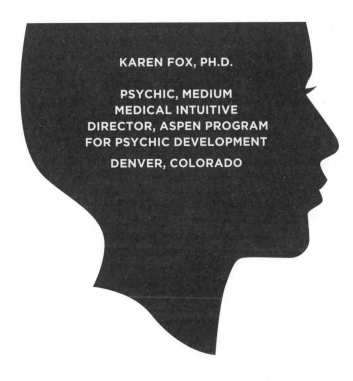

KAREN FOX, PH.D.

PSYCHIC, MEDIUM
MEDICAL INTUITIVE
DIRECTOR, ASPEN PROGRAM
FOR PSYCHIC DEVELOPMENT

DENVER, COLORADO

www.AspenProgram.com | www.PsychicIQ.com

Schiffer Publishing Ltd

4880 Lower Valley Road · Atglen, PA 19310

Other Schiffer Publications by Karen Fox, Ph.D.

Build Your Psychic Skills: The 90-Day Plan
ISBN: 978-0-7643-4561-6

Designed by Brenda McCallum
Cover design by Matt Goodman
Type set in Gotham/Garmond Pro

ISBN: 978-0-7643-4816-7
Printed in China

Published by Schiffer Publishing, Ltd.
4880 Lower Valley Road
Atglen, PA 19310
Phone: (610) 593-1777; Fax: (610) 593-2002
E-mail: Info@schifferbooks.com

For our complete selection of fine books on this and related subjects, please visit our website at www.schifferbooks.com. You may also write for a free catalog.

This book may be purchased from the publisher. Please try your bookstore first.

We are always looking for people to write books on new and related subjects. If you have an idea for a book, please contact us at proposals@schifferbooks.com.

Schiffer Publishing's titles are available at special discounts for bulk purchases for sales promotions or premiums. Special editions, including personalized covers, corporate imprints, and excerpts can be created in large quantities for special needs. For more information, contact the publisher.

Dedication

**To the students of the
Aspen Program for Psychic Development Denver, Colorado
www.AspenProgram.com**

Acknowledgments

This workbook is based on classes taught at the Aspen Program for Psychic Development. The program got its start at ISIS Books & Gifts, and owner Karen Charboneau-Harrison has been a tremendous supporter. ISIS is a beautiful store with a multiplicity of unique offerings (www.ISISBooks.com).

I have been fortunate to learn from a wonderful group of students at the Aspen Program. Each year, the program gets better because of their questions, struggles, and passion for learning. Special thanks, for their psychic exercise ideas, to Laura Earp, Jim Caudill, and the couple in the Lakewood Mentor Group. I also appreciate the many experiences of my students and clients, some of which I've included here.

Over the years, the Aspen Program has had a wonderful faculty and staff. I am grateful for their support and expertise, especially Sean Michael Morris, Marcia Stanfield, Lisa Lanyon, and Linda Vincent. Thank you Marcia for offering the idea "Running Your Clairs" and Lisa for allowing me to include her story and art expertise.

I am grateful for Ellen Capone, who taught me all about boundaries. She helped me find my inner writer and encouraged me to take risks that brought wonderful experiences into my life!

Many thanks for the patient editing done by Cat and for her listening to me talk about my work—over and over. (Sorry for not having enough time to be involved with your life interests.) I thank her for her insights and for challenging me to see things psychic from a unique perspective.

At Schiffer Publishing, special thanks to Dinah Roseberry and Chris McClure for getting my work accepted. It's a tremendous job to edit a workbook like this, and I appreciate the time-consuming detail it took Dinah to do this. In particular, I feel fortunate that she was personally engaged with the topic, and I loved her side comments about my work as she edited the manuscript. Thanks also for Chris' efforts to market this book.

I very much appreciate the exceptional expertise of the design team at Schiffer. This is not a typical book with the usual design requirements, and John Cheek, Matt Goodman, and Brenda McCallum took this book to another level with their creativity! I appreciate design supervisor John Cheek for orchestrating the production of so many concepts.

Matt Goodman's brain must have been exploding with ideas when he created the cover. Somehow he found a unique way to put it all together in a way that attracts the eye while providing tidbits of information to wet the appetite. Love all the colors; love the mind bursting with insights!

The cool, calming aqua waves that flow throughout the book along with the many beautiful graphics and relevant icons were the creation of Brenda McCallum. She took a choppy manuscript and turned it into an easy-to-use tool that makes sense. Her creativity and obvious connection with this work will make all the difference to the reader. I very much appreciate the head graphics at the start of each chapter. She captured the idea that the brain has so much more to offer us!

At last, but clearly not least, Pete Schiffer—without him, this book just wouldn't be here!

Student Evaluation of an Aspen Program Class:

This workbook is based on the Aspen Program for Psychic Development in Denver, Colorado. Here is what the author's students say about the curriculum included in this book:

What did you like the most about the class?

"Not feeling alone and knowing that I don't have to be perfect and that my psychic abilities can be learned—not just magically given to me, or that I wake up one day being 'all knowing.'"

"It is such an amazing thing you are doing. I am grateful to be a part of it. And thank you for your organization and detailed instruction. It is awesome."

"Well organized information. Answers the questions I was having. I feel more confident in my ability to get psychic information because of the variety of techniques given."

"Karen, Thank you soooooooooooo much! Thank you for sharing your gifts with us so we can develop ours! Thank you for all the work you did and for your extensive knowledge. It sure has made my development so much quicker and easier!"

"I appreciate all the information and handouts and your real-world experience and insights/advice. Love the organization of your materials!"

"Excellent organization. Loved the preparation. Really effective presentation style. Great content and delivery."

"You present the material in an understandable, sensible way. You don't tell us what to think or how to feel about things."

"My life has changed tremendously. I feel like I'm acknowledging a part of myself that I have forgotten about for so many years. My life has changed for the better, and I'm using my abilities in my everyday life. I've gotten a piece of myself back that has been gone since I was a child."

"I am so grateful to have found this program. Karen is an incredible instructor."

"Your encouragement and positive attitude helps with self-doubt and learning to TRUST this process."

"I am really enjoying these classes. Thanks for putting so much into it. I know this sounds cheesy, but you are seriously awesome!"

"I really miss the Aspen Program! There are NONE like it. None. Seriously."

Being psychic is a learned skill!

Contents

CHAPTER 1
So You Have a Hunch
What is Psychic Ability and Do You Have It?

Emily dragged her boyfriend Sam to her psychic reading session with me. It didn't take a psychic to know he was a skeptic. His arms were crossed over his chest, he slouched in the chair, and he had a look of disapproval on his face. When I correctly gave my client specifics about her life that I couldn't possibly have known, her boyfriend held on to his skepticism. I usually just let that attitude go. But, this time, I turned to him and said, "You aren't into any of this." Sam agreed, "No, I don't need to go to psychics. I'm intelligent enough that I don't need this."

I've heard comments like this before, and I'm impatient with the lack of curiosity people like this exhibit. What he didn't know was that I had a Ph.D.—I valued all aspects of the mind!

I put on my educator hat and asked, "So, you've never had a hunch about something that turned out to later happen?" I waited for him to remember that he'd had what every human has had: hunches.

"Well, I guess so," Sam replied with hesitation. He sat up a bit, as he told me about a work project, when he'd known the best steps to take because he'd had "a gut instinct." As he talked, Sam unfolded his arms and sat up further in his chair. He eagerly exclaimed that he had ultimately been right—and his team colleagues couldn't believe it. All skepticism left his face when we started using the words "hunch" and "gut instinct" in our conversation.

Invariably, when I shift the terminology from psychic to "hunch" or "gut instinct," most people can recount experiences like Sam's. You probably have had an immediate feeling upon walking into a room. Or perhaps you've gotten the feeling that if you turned your car to the right, you would find a parking space. Maybe there was a time when you had intuition about something happening to a loved one. All of these examples are attributed to the psychic sense. We regularly draw upon it, usually without recognizing that we are.

Psychic Learning Curve

Professional psychics I know view being "psychic" as something only professionals are capable of being, while "intuition" is for ordinary people—as if these were two separate things. I disagree. The psychic sense is a continuum of varying abilities, where occasional hunches are at the early stages of development. Increased psychic ability results from training and practice. Whatever you choose to call it, behind these experiences is the one psychic sense, with varying abilities to access it.

Everyone has a psychic sense—it's a natural, normal human instinct. It is not a "power" or a "gift," as popular television shows suggest. It's an inherent ability, a talent that can be integrated into your everyday life. Everyone can improve it. Like any skill, it just takes learning how to develop and use it. Yes, some individuals have greater talent. My sister plays the piano beautifully, and her husband can play a song after hearing it a couple times, but he doesn't read music. They both have a well-above-average ability.

But I can play the piano, too. It's not pretty, but I have played at church when the organist couldn't be there. My ability is functional enough, so that I can use it when needed. Likewise, everyone can increase their psychic capabilities to some extent—enough to give added help to their lives.

The first step in developing a strong psychic ability is to start acting on your hunches. It's perhaps the easiest step you can take right now to build a strong psychic sense!

How to Use This Workbook

This is your "class," where you can learn how to develop and use your psychic skills in your daily life. It contains lots of exercises and techniques that can be used with a partner or on your own. It's best to complete this workbook over a period of two-to-three months, rather than in one week, or infrequently, over a longer period of time. I recommend this based on my experience teaching students at the Aspen Program for Psychic Development.

Psychic skills are like muscles: the more you use them, the stronger they become. You wouldn't expect to go into a gym, lift some weights, and come out the first day, week, or month with a buff body. So be patient with yourself, and commit to a discipline of learning as you regularly use this material. In addition to this workbook, you might want to use my daily cards, *Build Your Psychic Skills: The 90-Day Plan*, (Schiffer Publishing, 2013).

Start in Chapter One by assessing the current level of your psychic ability. Make a note of the exercises and techniques you have difficulty with. Give more attention to these areas as you move through the workbook and you will find that your overall psychic ability increases.

One of the most frequent questions I get from students is, **"How do I know if what I am getting is psychic or whether it is coming from me?"** A major step in answering this question is to understand how the mind functions. Chapter Two covers this, so you can better know when you are using the psychic part of your mind and when the conscious and unconscious are getting in your way.

Psychic development requires a new way to learn. When you were in school, you worked at your studies by thinking, analyzing, and memorizing. If you didn't understand something, teachers expected you to work harder to learn the concept. Working hard to grow your psychic abilities just doesn't "work." I will show you how to allow your mind to give you insights.

You do not need a particular religious belief or world view to be psychic. People from all walks of life are psychic. Things psychic have for too long been the province of metaphysical, New Age groups. You do not have to embrace any particular way of thinking to develop your psychic abilities.

The basic characteristics of the psychic sense are the "clairs," a French word meaning "clear." For example, clairvoyance is "clear seeing" or psychic seeing ("voyance"). In Chapter Three, you will develop six "clairs." You are already using them now, and you likely have a strong and weak "clair." You will benefit by using the exercises provided to strengthen all your "clairs."

Also in Chapter Three, you will use what you are learning to gain insights into a question that is relevant in your life now. Look for "Answers to Your Question" when you see this graphic ▶

Use the same question each time you see this graphic so you have plenty of data to use at the end of Chapter Four when you will be provided with a procedure to assess your psychic answers.

I give my students a variety of ways to develop their psychic sense, so they can choose what works best for them. Chapter Four gives you seven approaches to psychic development with lots of techniques, exercises, and games. You can easily integrate the ideas in this chapter into your daily life.

Students are often plagued by blocks or impediments to their psychic abilities. I have blocks; everyone has blocks. It's called being human. In Chapter Five, you will learn to identify those blocks and develop resources for moving through them. You will find that, as you open yourself to this innate sense, you will likely be challenged to grow personally as well. The degree to which you are willing to explore your inner psychological makeup and increase your self-knowledge, the stronger and more accessible your psychic sense will be.

Perhaps the biggest block to accessing psychic ability is that we live in a society that doesn't value things psychic, so we are never taught how to develop this part of our minds. When I was younger, psychics told me that I could do what they did. I knew I had the ability, but to sit down in front of someone and give a psychic reading...that terrified me. I figured that if I really had these abilities, I would have somehow been magically giving psychic readings by the age of ten!

Finally, one psychic said it in a way that made sense to me. "Karen, the only difference between you and me is practice." Practice? That meant I could *learn* how to be psychic. Today, that idea may seem obvious to you, but it didn't back then to me. Some psychics promoted the idea that only a few special people were psychic, and television has perpetuated this erroneous idea. That's ridiculous! This workbook does what any school teacher does: it teaches you how to understand and develop skills—in this case, psychic skills.

This workbook explains a method for both developing and using your psychic ability during brief time periods throughout your day. If you use the workbook daily over the next two-to-three months, you will discover that you have psychic ability when you need it. Chapter Six and the back of this workbook provide you with cards you can copy and take with you, so your abilities will be there when you want them.

In these challenging times, it helps to have an edge—and your own psychic sense can give you that. Your psychic ability is an important part of being a well-rounded person. It can help you make decisions. Your psychic insights may bring out issues or information that you would otherwise not have considered. Why not use the full capacities of your mind—both your analytical mind and your psychic sense?

Conrad Hilton, creator of the Hilton Hotel fortune, wrote in his autobiography that he used his intuition to get property at the lowest bid. Backers referred to his talent as "Connie's hunches," after he made a killing on bonds.

> I've been accused more than once of playing hunches. Since I suppose I do and it sounds so mysterious, a little like following a Ouija board or gazing into a crystal ball, and since I further believe most people have them, whether they follow them or not, I've tried to figure out what's in a hunch. I think the other name for hunch is intuition.
>
> —Conrad Hilton
> Be My Guest, 1957, page 196

As "Connie" exclaimed—we all have it! His experience guides us to listen "in a sort of inside silence 'til something clicks, and I feel a right answer."

Why develop and use your psychic sense? Most of my students want to develop their skills to obtain added insights for their lives. Some are plagued by having so much natural ability, they just want to gain control over it. A few go on to become professional psychics, mediums, business intuitives, animal communicators, psychic life coaches, and medical intuitives. This workbook will help you turn intermittent hunches and gut instincts into a strong psychic sense, so it is reliably there when you need additional insights for your life.

Breathe …

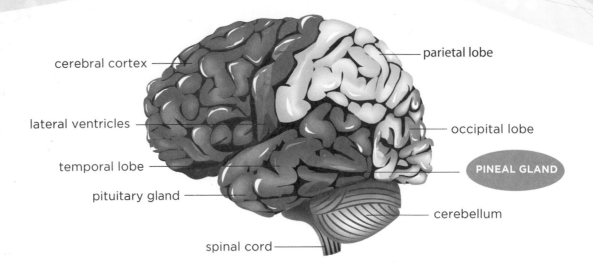

cerebral cortex

parietal lobe

lateral ventricles

occipital lobe

temporal lobe

PINEAL GLAND

pituitary gland

cerebellum

spinal cord

Exercise:
Start opening your psychic ability now!

THIRD-EYE/PSYCHIC EYE BREATHING

Do this off and on throughout your day, except when driving or other times when you need to pay attention. If it seems silly at first, just pretend.

- **Get comfortable and relax.** Take a deep breath, and let it out with a sigh. Open your jaw a bit at the hinge; feel your shoulders relax; sense your body releasing into your chair or where you are standing.

- **Put your attention at the center of your forehead.** Pretend you are breathing in and out of your third-eye located at the center of your forehead. See and feel the breath going in and out of the middle of your forehead. You might sense a pressure, tingling, or a slight headache. After some practice, discomfort will likely not occur.

- **Breathe with your pineal gland**. When you can clearly feel the center of your forehead breathing, move your awareness into your brain and breathe with the pineal gland. It is in the center of your brain and is the size of a grain of rice. Your awareness will find it, and you will get a sense of its physical and energetic characteristics. Continue breathing, feeling the third-eye open and expand.

- **Say to yourself (or out loud), "I am psychic."** This affirmative statement works with the unconscious mind to open your innate psychic sense. Say this while breathing with your third-eye.

- **Ground yourself** after this exercise by visualizing the door to your third-eye closing, and then breathe with your feet and the Earth.

Start making notes in a journal about your experiences with psychic development. Include your dreams and artwork, too. Writing and reflecting on this process will make all the difference in your learning. The journal can be on an electronic device or a paper book.

Carry a small notebook where you can record in-the-moment insights and synchronicities.

NOTES

NOTES

CHAPTER 2

Getting Started
Know Your Psychic Sense

It's the first class at the Aspen Program. Students are eager to get started. After the welcome and introductions, I discuss two major concerns I hear from students about their psychic abilities:

1. HOW DO I KNOW THAT WHAT I AM GETTING IS REALLY PSYCHIC?
2. WHAT DO I DO WHEN I'M BLOCKED AND CAN'T GET ANYTHING PSYCHICALLY?

"So," I say to them, "that's what we're going to deal with now." I motion to the students with my hands, "Stand up. Pick up your chair, turn it around, and sit down. Keep your eyes open."

I continue with the lecture, telling them I understand their need to know that what they are getting is *really, really* psychic and not just something they've made up. What that is *really* about is the need to be right. That's because society regards psychics as fakes: what cannot be proven cannot be real. Our need to be right about our psychic insights is often a fear of being wrong and perceived as a fake.

Part of human nature is being wrong at times. At the beginning of learning anything, you may be wrong—particularly when it comes to being psychic, because you probably haven't yet learned how the psychic sense functions. No one does anything perfectly when they first start. If you are willing to be wrong as you develop your psychic skills, you will learn more. I had a boss who once said to me after I had made a big mistake, "Karen, if you're not making mistakes, you're not doing anything!" Great boss!

So, I tell my students and you: If you don't allow yourself to be wrong as you move through this material, you aren't learning how to develop the full capacity of your psychic sense. Giving yourself permission to be wrong provides you with opportunities to learn from your mistakes. Don't let the need to be right trip you up.

My students are still facing in the opposite direction. They can't see me as I speak. Some will tell me later they were distracted by what they were looking at in the back of the room. Others found it awkward to learn when they couldn't see me talking.

With the students still sitting with their backs to me, I move on to talk about those pesky blocks that get in the way when one wants to be psychic. I'll tell you a secret: professional psychics have blocks, too. But professionals should know how to deal with them.

I will teach you to recognize and move through any blocks you may have, and how to know that what you are getting is coming from a psychic source. First, it helps to understand how the mind works, so you will better know where the information is coming from and how to get past the stuck parts.

I draw on the board the three parts of the mind and list their characteristics. I pause for ten seconds, counting in silence each second with my fingers.

Then I ask the students, "What's going through your head right now?" No one responds. I usually have to repeat the question multiple times, asking again for anyone to speak up. It's as if they don't have permission to speak unless they can *see* the person asking the question.

A student finally mumbles, "It's weird not seeing you." Others chime in, "I feel like I'm missing out on something because I can't see you." "I wanted to know what you were writing on the board. I think I know, but I'm not sure." "I got bored, so my mind wandered."

I invite the bewildered students to turn their chairs around and sit facing me.

"Welcome to *psychic development*," I say. "This is what being psychic can feel like."

That's what learning anything can be like in the beginning. You won't always be able to see, feel, or touch things psychically. What you get psychically isn't always clear and easy to understand—at first. That's a standard in our society that nothing is real unless you SEE it. You have to set that notion aside, just as a person recently blinded has to learn new ways of operating in the physical world.

The first step in learning how the psychic sense operates is to understand how the mind operates. Later in this chapter, we'll go over the characteristics of the conscious and unconscious minds and how they can interfere with the psychic part of your mind. These parts of your mind are not separate. They all work in conjunction with each other. But it helps to separate them into models so you can better understand how your psychic sense works and put more emphasis on it.

You also need new ways of learning. You have to allow your mind to give you information. I'll give you suggestions for how to do this, so you can strengthen your psychic sense. Finally, this chapter includes a list of what a healthy psychic sense looks like. It will help you to know where you are going with your abilities while using this workbook.

Create Your Package!

You need a strong "package" for your psychic abilities to thrive. The package is just as important as your level of psychic ability. It's about staying grounded and centered and having good boundaries and ethics. It also includes the ability to disconnect and to get past being stuck.

Throughout the workbook, you will get quick tips to create your "package." Look for. Don't skip these—they only takes a few minutes to do, and in that little bit of time, you will be creating a strong container for your abilities.

(This is covered in greater detail in Chapter 5, if you think you need it sooner.)

TIP FOR GOOD BOUNDARIES:	How is your body feeling? Smile. How is your body feeling now? When you are aware of your body, it's easier to sense and then create healthy energy boundaries.

1 Self-Assessment of Your Current Abilities

A good place to begin is to know where you are now with your psychic abilities. You are somewhere on the psychic learning curve—everyone is. The following pages will provide you with tools to begin thinking about where your starting point will be.

As you complete the forms, use the process to explore what your psychic abilities are now, as well as when you were a child. Please *do not* compare your level of psychic skills with others. That will only get in your way. You are naturally psychic, and this workbook gives you the tools to improve this inherent ability.

Return to the assessments over time to track your progress. (When my students went back to them, they were surprised at how much their psychic sense had grown.)

Self-Assessment:

Put a check by the characteristics that apply to you now or when you were a child.

CHARACTERISTICS OF PSYCHIC PEOPLE/KIDS

☒ 1. Sensitive to <u>noise</u>, the taste of foods, smells/odors, certain colors or color combinations, or touch.

☒ 2. Don't like to be overstimulated. Can be easily overwhelmed (crowds, noise).

☐ 3. Allergies and upper respiratory problems.

☐ 4. Don't like to be around electrical equipment. Light bulbs go off around you.

☒ 5. Don't like to be in crowds.

☐ 6. Slow to connect with others, particularly in childhood. You tend to participate in group activities only after getting to know the people, the environment, and the dynamics.

☐ 7. When you enter a room, you usually check out the feel of the atmosphere and people.

☐ 8. Refuse to go near a particular person, room, or building, particularly in childhood.

☒ 9. Feel the emotions of others as if these emotions were your own; feel responsible for others' emotions. May overreact, particularly as a child. You have a greater need to resolve emotional conflicts because of this sensitivity towards others' emotions. It's more difficult for you to let go of emotions (yours and others). May cry easily.

☑ 10. Don't like conflict. Have a strong sense of justice and unfairness. You want to "right" wrongs.

☑ 11. You seem to read family/friend's mind. You know what others want before they ask.

❑ 12. Aware that something is happening to a family member or close friend.

❑ 13. Seem to know when someone is ill.

☑ 14. When you are alone in a room, you feel it is full or you have the feeling that spirits are in the room. Feelings of being watched that is not related to a mental disorder.

❑ 15. You know the personalities of deceased family members you have never met. As a child, you recognize deceased family members in photographs.

❑ 16. Take on the mannerisms and speech of other people.

❑ 17. Animals and young children follow you or want to be around you.

❑ 18. See/feel energy in a room, in your hands, around others (even if not colorful as in the aura/energy field that is around every living thing).

❑ 19. Active dream life with vivid colors; flying dreams; fall out of bed a lot as a child; premonition dreams; aware that you are dreaming.

❑ 20. Talk with and/or feel nature, particularly in childhood.

❑ 21. Objects move around you, particularly in childhood.

❑ 22. Had an "imaginary" friend or animal in childhood.

❑ 23. As a child, fear of the dark or "a boogey man" in your room at night.

❑ 24. Talked about a past life as a child.

❑ 25. Artistic, creative, imaginative.

❑ 26. Think outside the box.

❑ 27. Hear someone calling your name, but no one is (in our reality).

☑ 28. Good sense of direction.

☑ 29. Experiences of déjà-vu.

☑ 30. Family members exhibit intuitive or psychic abilities.

Discussion:

You are psychic even if you only checked a few of the characteristics. It's a beginning list based on my experiences with students, and you may want to include your own examples. The major reason I include this is to get you to think about how you may have exhibited psychic ability as a child.

Psychic kids are often teased as being too sensitive. They often literally feel other people's emotions (#9) and don't like crowds (#5) because of it. If only someone could have said something like, "Yes, you are particularly sensitive, and that can be a good thing. It means you have the ability to understand things that others often don't. Let me tell you how to handle this, so you don't feel so overwhelmed." This message validates that it's good to be psychically sensitive and, as children mature, these abilities can be honed to access the greater capacities of the mind.

Throughout time, children have had some level of psychic sensitivity. But it is not valued and so it is lost. Psychically gifted children are often stressed by not understanding what is happening to them. They could be helped to strengthen these skills if we included psychic development as a regular part of their education.

My interest in teaching was fueled, in part, by an experience I had at an annual gallery reading at Halloween. Many cultures celebrate this time of year to honor family members on "the other side." Picnics are held at gravesites, and some use this time to communicate with their loved ones. They believe that the veil between our world and the spirit world is thinner at this time of year, so it is easier to make connections between the two realms.

As I read the spirits in the gallery, my attention was suddenly drawn to the young girl on my right who was sitting with her mother. Without thinking, I blurted out, "You see dead people." She nodded her head slowly up and down. She seemed surrounded by lots of spirits, but one stood out. Behind her was a spirit who was dripping wet. Again, without thinking that I should temper my comments when talking to a six-year old, I said, "There is a man behind you, and he is dripping wet." She said she knew he was there. I continued on, talking with her mother about how to assist her child. I was just about to go on to the next person, when it came to me to say one more thing.

"How are you feeling?" The little girl quietly said, "Confused."

And I knew immediately that it was the dripping wet spirit who was confused. The little girl had taken on his feelings as her own. That happened a lot to me as a child and young adult and to many psychic people I know. We need to assist our children with their psychic sensitivities, if only so they won't be confused.

Self-Assessment:

The items below contribute to creating a strong psychic sense. Using the scale below, put a number by each item that indicates where you are currently.

FOUNDATION FOR PSYCHIC DEVELOPMENT

1	2	3	4	5
Doesn't relate to me at all		Applies somewhat, but not a major part of my life or identity		This is definitely me!

[5] 1. **I have the ability to quiet my mind:** I can turn off my mind chatter when I want (most of the time). I have experience with meditation, hypnosis, relaxation CDs, or other techniques to quiet self-talk, so I am able to listen to my inner voice.

[5] 2. **I am body aware:** I can tune into and get insights from my body. I have experience with massage, energywork, Yoga, Tai Chi, Qi Gong, running/walking, or other techniques, so I am able to connect with my body.

[5] 3. **I am psychologically healthy:** I am aware when I am emotionally triggered, and I have tools to move through difficult times. I have healthy boundaries. I am introspective about myself. I reflect about my life and have ways to process life experiences. I have experience with individual therapy, group work, retreats, or other approaches to heal psychological trauma and childhood issues.

[5] 4. **I spend time alone:** I make time during my day or week to be alone with myself. (You will find it easier to access your psychic abilities if you regularly spend quiet time alone.)

[5] 5. **I am creative:** I enjoy expressing my creativity through art, crafts, writing, drama/acting, music, dance, or other avenues. Creativity is a regular part of my life.

[2] 6. **I work with my dreams:** There are times when I don't do dreamwork, but I can usually remember my dreams when I want. I have gotten past the stage where most of my dreams seem confusing.

[5] 7. **I am curious:** I view myself as a lifelong learner, and I am open to new ideas. Whatever beliefs I currently hold about the meaning and purpose of life, I am open to exploring this, and I respect that others may see the world differently from me.

Self-Assessment:

Below are experiences that relate to general psychic abilities, medical intuition, and spirit mediumship. Circle the number that most describes your experiences. Be sure to return to this in three to six months, and see how your abilities have grown.

DATE: 8/18/2020

1	2	3	4	5
Not Much		Sometimes		A Lot

My Psychic Abilities Now:

[3] When I go into a place for the first time, I can sense the energy in the room.

[2] Thoughts/ideas pop into my head, and I know they aren't mine.
Sometimes lots of information just comes to me.

[1] I have dreams that later come true in my waking life.

[1] I can have lucid dreams where I am aware that I am dreaming.

[1] I see, sense, or feel auras (the energy field around people).

[3] I have had premonitions about the future.

[2] I am so connected to a friend or family member that we pickup on each other's thoughts, and I've been aware when something important is happening to them.

[2] I have had déjà vu experiences.

[3] I am clairvoyant (psychic seeing).

[3] I am clairaudient (psychic hearing or thoughts).

[5] I am clairsentient (pickup on people's emotions or sense energy).

[3] I am claircognizant (I just immediately know).

My Medical Intuitive Abilities Now:

[5] I can easily sense my own body.

[1] I feel other people's health problems in my body. (Note: It's best not to allow this to happen; you can learn to read health without feeling it in your body.)

[1] I get psychic information about the health of family members, friends, or others I'm close to.

[1] I have known when someone is about to die or have a baby.

[1] I do hands-on energywork, and I can easily sense energy in other's bodies.

My Spirit Medium Abilities Now:

[\ ] I sense spirits:

    ['] See with my naked eye

    [\ ] See with my inner, psychic eye

    [\ ] Feel their presence

    [\ ] "Hear" them talk with me

[\ ] Spirits have moved objects near me.

[\ ] I have heard my name called or thought I did, and it didn't come from a living person; maybe it happened during a dream.

[3] When alone, I feel like someone is watching me and/or the room feels full.

[3] Deceased family members or others visited me in spirit or in my dreams.

Create Your Package!

TIP FOR GOOD BOUNDARIES: How are you feeling emotionally right now?
Go wash your hands.
Check your feelings again.

List Your Personal Strengths:

This is not about your psychic abilities. List below what you think are the positive characteristics in your personality. Examples: Dedicated, ethical, overcame life difficulties, responsible. Your personal strengths are an important part of the "package," so that you can effectively use your psychic abilities.

empathetic, good listener, responsible, always seeing life experiences as playing for the best for all that are involved, go w/ the flow of the universe, grateful for my life + family + environment, curious, adventurous, straightforward, loved+supported by Sheri, Noah, Gabriel + family + friends

WRITE ABOUT THE MOST SIGNIFICANT LIFE PROBLEM OR ISSUE YOU ARE EXPERIENCING NOW AND HOW YOU ARE ADDRESSING IT.

As you develop your psychic skills using this workbook, continue to explore how this problem/issue may be influencing your psychic development. This is NOT about your psychic abilities—it's about your life.

Problems are a part of the human condition. What's important is how you deal with them and that you have resources to draw upon. If you want to be more psychic, you've got to deal with your "stuff." We all have leftover stuff from life experiences. As you open your psychic abilities, some of that will likely present itself to you. The more you are willing to recognize and are capable of dealing with your own emotional problems and development, the better your psychic abilities will be. Psychic development involves personal development.

Not a life problem => more creating how I can serve, help, synthesize my interest to be of service to others - ple, animals, plants, mother earth AND in so doing create an income to help with our life style.

WHAT CONCERNS YOU ABOUT COMMUNICATING WITH SPIRITS AND/OR DEVELOPING YOUR PSYCHIC ABILITIES?

Do you have a fear of spirits? Are you concerned that you will not be able to close down your psychic abilities when you want to? How do you deal with these issues now?

(Not everyone has fears or anxieties about spirits and psychic abilities—but the media sure has contributed to increasing fear of the spirit world.)

Yes - feel a little fearful abt communicating w/ spirits. NOT my Dad - but I really haven't been approached or have had / experiences w/ spirits.

WHY DO YOU WANT TO DEVELOP YOUR PSYCHIC SENSE?

Below are the reasons people have given me for wanting to develop their psychic abilities. It's helpful to know why you are spending time with this workbook—to keep you motivated and better able to accomplish your goals. Your reasons may change, and that's okay.

Check all the reasons below that apply to you:

[✓] Communicate with spirit guides.

[ ] Make better decisions.

[✓] Use abilities on the job.

[✓] Improve my health.

[✓] Connect with my body.

[✓] Enhance my creativity.

[✓] Improve my finances.

[✓] Insight into life direction or purpose.

[✓] Access the realm of ideas and inventions.

[✓] Help children with their psychic abilities.

[✓] Communicate with people in spirit who have died.

[✓] Compelled to do something with the psychic abilities I have always had.

[✓] Have a balanced, holistic life with good access to the full capacity of my mind.

[ ] Validate the experiences I've had—that I'm not crazy.

[✓] Be a professional psychic, medium, medical intuitive, animal communicator, or other psychic professional.

[ ] I'm not sure yet.

[ ] Other.

_____

_____

_____

_____

_____

_____

_____

_____

_____

_____

_____

_____

_____

_____

_____

_____

_____

_____

Start meditating now.

Ugh! I know, I know; you don't have time or maybe you just don't want to. Try this:

Off and on throughout your day and evening, use this mind relaxation technique. Do it for as long as you like, even just a minute. Commit to using this technique daily for the next 90 days.

Take in three long, deep breaths, and let them out with an audible sigh.

Open your jaw at the hinge, relax your shoulders, and release your belly.

Observe your breath, coming back to your breath if your mind wanders. Do this for as long as you prefer. Then go on with your day.

Exercise:

**WRITE A STORY, LET IT FLOW WITHOUT THINKING ABOUT IT—
ALLOW THE STORY LINE TO POP INTO YOUR MIND.**

Start with these words:
Once upon a time, on a dark and stormy night…

I was in my bed sleeping & was woken up by the cracks thunder & lightening lighting up my room. It scared me. Arty was sleeping & I wanted to jump in bed w/ me. I was alone & he was not there. Leo awake on the bed from the noisey thunder. I let Arty on the bed too & the 3 of us hung out loving each other watching the room lit up & listening to the cracks of the thunder. It lasted for about an hour. We all finally fell asleep & wore up to sunshine & coolness in the air. We got up brushed my teeth, fed the animals & made some coffee. We all went outside to greet the morning. Called Suzy & told him all our night. I felt really grateful to have that experience w/ Arty & Leo. It was a sweet hr together that may never happen again.

Exercise Discussion:

I write and think like a left-brainer. I wrote government regulations and computer manuals in my twenties and thirties, and I find myself comfortable in that analytical, logical, methodical mind space. So in my forties, when I was working on my doctorate in sociology at Syracuse University, I was surprised to meet a fellow grad student who had done his master's in creative writing. I was using "narratives" (academic code word for "stories") in my work, but I didn't understand why a fiction writer was in the sociology department. He told me about a book he was writing, and I asked how it ended. He said that he didn't know.

What?! Even J. K. Rowling knew how the *Harry Potter* story would end. Having written few creative pieces, except for the typical poetry of adolescence, pre-planned outlines are what drive my writing. I write the beginning, support in the middle, and then end with a summary. But when I removed the shackles of my logical-computer manual thinking and ventured into his creative wonderland, I understood his point:

IDEAS JUST COME TO YOU.
AND THAT'S HOW THE PSYCHIC SENSE FUNCTIONS—IT JUST COMES.

In the first class I teach at the Aspen Program, I ask students to write a story like you just did. It's the best way to teach how the psychic sense works. When you can get in that space to let the words and ideas and images pop into your mind, you will better understand what that space feels like when receiving psychic insights.

Let insights come to you—that's how the psychic sense works.

Start Focusing on Your Dreams

Dreams are one of the best sources of psychic information. Dreams are also one of the best ways to improve your psychic abilities.

Place paper, pencil, and light by the bed to record your dreams immediately upon waking.

While falling asleep, repeat a suggestion to remember your dreams, such as, "I remember my dreams." See yourself writing your dreams down when you wake up in the morning.

Don't move upon waking. Keep your eyes closed. Review the night's dreams. Slowly move your body as you get your paper and pen, and write your dreams in an outline format. Fill in the details then, if you have time, or do it later.

Write down something, anything! No matter how seemingly insignificant, write about your nighttime dreams. Whether it is a few words, a phrase, one sentence, or just how you felt upon waking. Consistency in dreamwork brings improved results.

You will receive instruction to interpret your dreams in Chapter Four and whenever you see this moon graphic. ▶

"HOW DO I KNOW IF WHAT I AM GETTING IS PSYCHIC OR IT IS COMING FROM ME?"

A major step in answering the question is to understand how the mind functions, so that you know what part of your mind the insights are coming from. The mind can be viewed as having three parts:

1. Conscious, or thinking mind
2. Unconscious, or ego-need mind
3. Creative/imaginative/expanded awareness, or psychic mind

Our minds really don't have three neat distinctions. We likely draw upon these aspects of the mind holistically, as they function together. Unfortunately, we have been taught to focus primarily on the conscious, thinking mind. Some attention has also been given to dealing with unconscious psychological issues. But we have never placed sufficient focus on the psychic aspects of our mind. The first budget items cut in schools are art and music, both part of that creative function where the psychic sense lies.

The psychic sense operates through, what I like to call, the "expanded awareness." It is a function of the imagination, and that's why creative people such as artists and musicians are often more psychic. Psychic awareness is with us all the time—we are always using it to some extent, as in a hunch or gut instinct. It is more accessible when we set aside the conscious, thinking mind, relax our bodies, and address unconscious blocks. Then we can better hear our inner voice, our psychic sense.

When I was developing my psychic ability, I called a mentor and asked what many students ask me today. "How do I know if what I'm getting is just my imagination?" A seasoned psychic, Mary replied, "You are asking the wrong question. Your psychic ability is part of your imagination. The question should be, 'How do you know if it's fantasy—that you are making it up?'" If you are making up the images and story line, it's fantasy. The imagination is part of our creative expression where ideas, images, and innovation just pop into our minds—that's the psychic sense!

The **conscious mind** thinks, analyzes, interprets, and decides. When you attempt to find information—to go looking or searching for it—you are using your conscious mind. Alternatively, the psychic mind simply allows information to come to you. Our society values conscious, analytical ways of knowing; and we, therefore, rely heavily upon this. You will need to be aware when you are using your conscious mind, so you can set aside that way of knowing.

The **unconscious mind** is the storehouse of our beliefs. You might be surprised at the beliefs you hold that lie hidden in your unconscious mind, such as the message that was sent to most of us growing up that psychic information is not credible. Perhaps you had a psychic experience that scared you. It could have been sensing a spirit or knowing that something bad was going to happen in the future. The trauma of these experiences may be stored in your unconscious mind as a belief that things psychic are scary. You may consciously want to develop your psychic abilities, but your unconscious beliefs and experiences may get in your way—because the unconscious mind has more ability to override the desires of our conscious mind than we generally recognize.

If you work on developing your psychic abilities and you haven't seen improvement after three to six months, you may have blocks getting in your way (some of which may be unconscious). Suggestions for addressing blocks are in Chapter 5. If you are feeling stuck and frustrated before you get to that chapter, flip ahead and work with the material sooner.

The ego is another unconscious aspect of the mind that can get in your way. We all have ego needs—the need to feel good about ourselves, to be appreciated, to be wanted, and to be heard. When our ego self is unhealthy, we might have so much self-doubt that we undercut our ability to learn and grow. It's natural to have some self-doubt when first learning something. But too much self-doubt and self-criticism may indicate low self-esteem that needs to be addressed, so that you can fully access your psychic abilities. The way to know whether low self-esteem is getting in your way is to practice. If self-doubt or other blocks still plague you after three to six months of dedicated practice, it's time to look deeper within yourself.

Another unhealthy ego need is the need to feel superior to other people, which is often just the other side of the low self-esteem coin. If you have a need to feel superior, the psychic insights you get may be shaped by this ego need. You might have more difficulty setting aside the conscious, advice-giving part of you. In my opinion, when giving a psychic reading, about eighty percent of what is said to a client should come from a psychic source—not counseling, opinion, or advice. Clients (and you!) are best served if this type of support is found from friends, family members, and trusted advisors.

Psychics and students of psychic development often struggle with issues of superiority and self-doubt. That's human. But to have effective psychic abilities that we can draw upon to assist ourselves (or others) with life, we must be willing to self-reflect about our psychological makeup and take steps to develop a healthy, strong ego.

Create Your Package!

TIP FOR GOOD BOUNDARIES:

Put your hand on your belly, and be with it. How does your belly feel?

If you have a wooden bowl, put it over your belly for about five minutes, while focusing your attention there. If you don't have one handy, just place both hands there instead.

Now, how does it feel?

The **psychic mind** doesn't go looking for information like the conscious mind does. Images, thoughts, and ideas just pop into your mind. That's when you know that what you are getting is most likely psychic—it just pops into your mind. As you learn to set aside your conscious mind, while using your psychic sense, your abilities will get stronger, and you won't have to think as much about which aspect of your mind your insights are coming from.

The more you know your own mind and how it works, the better your psychic abilities will be, and the better you can answer the question, "Is what I'm getting psychic?"

Below is a list of characteristics of the three aspects of the mind. Study the chart and, as you go through the day, ask yourself what part of your mind you are using at any given moment. Where are your ideas coming from; how is your mind processing information? This self-reflection will not only add to your psychic development, but you will also increase your critical thinking skills.

Being psychic is about knowing your own mind.
The end goal of psychic development is effective use of your mind.

Psychic, Conscious, Unconscious

Get familiar with your mind ~ Know where your insights are coming from.

Psychic Mind

- *Receives* insights; allows
- Insights "pop" into your mind
- Psychic insights usually come when you are "in the zone," as in meditation

Conscious Mind

- Thinks
- Analyzes
- Interprets
- Looks for insights
- Advice, opinion, counseling
- Decides/chooses

Our society places primary value on thinking, analyzing mental processes, so we are heavily biased in favor of this way of getting insights. When doing psychic work, the conscious mind has to stay out. Only later, should you use your conscious mind to evaluate your psychic insights.

Unconscious Mind

- Beliefs
- Stored memory
- Effects of trauma
- What gets triggered
- Unhealthy ego needs from unresolved stuff

Low self-esteem that shows up as excessive self-doubt and fear or as the need to feel superior to others can interfere with accessing psychic abilities and get in the way of communicating what you get psychically.

A Grounding Technique—
Breathe with Your Feet and the Earth

Put your awareness inside your feet. Be present there for a moment. Then pretend that the only part of your body that is breathing is your feet. Do this for a few minutes or until you feel connected to your feet. Then move your awareness deep inside the Earth. Be present there for a moment; feel the Earth breathing. Then synchronize your feet breathing with the breath of the Earth. Breathe with your feet and the Earth for as long as you'd like.

Breathe ...

Exercise:

Solve these equations:

$135 - 66 =$ Find "x": $3x + 5 + 2x = 12 - 4$ Find "x": $X = {}^2\sqrt{121}$

It's the first day of class. Students are eager to learn how to be psychic. I put these equations on the board, ask my students to solve them, and I leave the room. I don't know what goes on in the room while I'm gone. But when I return, there is some under-the-breath chuckling. "Has Karen lost it," they wonder. "What does this have to do with psychic development?" They tell me: "I can't solve that last one, and I'm not sure I remember how to do the second one."

I break the tension: "Why in the world would you expect to solve the equations, if you were not taught how to solve them?"

After years of teaching students to be psychic, I finally got what was getting in their way—and I don't want it to get in *your* way. You wouldn't take a math exam before you learned how to do math. So again I say: don't focus on getting it right as you move through this workbook. Students come to class, and they are so concerned about failing at being psychic that they don't allow themselves to be taught. You aren't here to demonstrate how psychic you are now, although you may be very psychic already. The purpose of this workbook is to learn—use it to learn—not to prove you are psychic.

Is it bugging you that I haven't given you the answers to the equations? Do you want the proof that you can do two or three of the equations? If so, you missed the point.

I over-emphasize the focus on "getting it right" because I've seen this concern get in many a student's way. They want to jump to being psychic without learning the "how-to" and the components of the psychic sense. Sure, you can develop abilities without knowing how the psychic sense functions—just practice until you get better. But you can only take your abilities so far, because what's missing is developing the whole psychic sense—not just the parts of it that you are naturally good at.

There wasn't much available to help me when I developed my abilities. I just did it—practice was about all I had. That's what most of us did "back then." Practice is important, but understanding the theory and function of the psychic sense will make you better at being psychic. And when I figured this out, so that I could teach students, my own abilities deepened, and my readings got better.

Psychic Learning Curve

$135 - 66 =$ Find "x": $3x + 5 + 2x = 12 - 4$ Find "x": $X = {}^2\sqrt{121}$

Remember that right now you are somewhere on the psychic learning curve. Think of the psychic sense as having a continuum of skill level. Wherever your ability is now, you can develop it further. Your mind already knows how to be psychic—you just need to learn how to let it do its job so that you can move further along that continuum and obtain stronger psychic abilities. Allow yourself to get better by:

1. Learning how the psychic sense functions

2. Allowing yourself to fail

3. Learning from your failures

Exercise:

Get a deck of regular playing cards
Place the 10 of Hearts face up
Place the 10 of Clubs face up

- Shuffle the deck. Take the top card (face down) from the deck, and hold it. Allow the color (black or red) to quickly come to you. I haven't taught you about the "clairs" yet, but use the recording sheet on the following page to track how you get the color: by seeing, hearing or getting a thought, immediate knowing, or sensing the energy or emotion of the color. Don't overthink this. Just let the color come to you, and place a "tick" mark by the "clair" you think you used to get the color.

- Then place the card face down near the 10 of Hearts or Clubs depending on what color you psychically got. Don't look at it. Stay focused on the experience; stay away from evaluating how well you are doing.

- Pay attention to thoughts that come up as you do this exercise. A list is provided on the next page. Every time one of these thoughts arises, place a "tick" mark by the thought.

- "Read" about half of the deck, and then stop and read the next paragraph.

As you did the exercise, did you find that, at times, you got a bit anxious, wondering if you were getting the colors right? Perhaps anxiety was building. When this happens, or other thoughts keep entering into your mind, try shuffling the deck, as if you are erasing the thoughts or anxious feelings.

Continue reading the cards until you have completed the entire deck. When you have finished, don't look at the cards. Come back to the workbook and keep reading.

Pick up all the cards without looking at the colors, and shuffle the deck. I hear groans every time I ask my students to do this. They really want to know how they did. You'll probably want to peek, too. But you will miss a very important part of developing your psychic abilities if you look to see how well you did.

I was playing around with the cards one day, checking how I did each time. I did pretty well, getting 60 to 70 percent correct. But I noticed self-doubt creeping into my head, and sometimes this would get in the way. That's when I decided to not look at all. Instead, I focused on those annoying thoughts of self-doubt.

Focus on your process of being psychic and not on what you get right/wrong. Get to the point where you don't care how good you are. Focusing on where did it come from, what "clair" am I using—am I using my conscious mind, how am I being psychic?—is much more important than being right every time. The most important learning opportunity involves finding out *how you got what you got*, not whether you were right. Focus on:

WHAT'S GOING ON IN MY MIND AS I AM BEING PSYCHIC?

This exercise will give you the opportunity to explore how your thoughts affect your psychic ability. Not only will you learn how to set aside unproductive thoughts, so you can be more psychic, but your mind will get stronger as your self-doubt decreases. If your self-doubt doesn't decrease, that may be more about your inner psychological makeup than your psychic abilities.

As you get to know your internal thinking process better, you may discover unique tools for getting past the times when you are stuck. That's when I figured out that shuffling the deck cleared those thoughts, so I could more easily keep reading the cards.

I also learned another technique for getting unstuck. I used distraction, and I got better. Shuffling the cards is one distraction, but I also watched a favorite television show, as I psychically read the cards. When interfering thoughts got in my way, I focused on the show. Sometimes I watched the show at the same time I read a card or two.

I did this exercise for about two weeks without looking, until I just didn't care about how I was doing. I found that I had shifted from the want to be right to a focus on how I got in my own way, and I was learning to let that roll off my back. I was learning how to allow myself to be psychic—even more psychic.

And, when I finally looked at how I was doing weeks later, I got them all correct except for five cards. Trust me when I tell you that in the beginning of developing your psychic abilities, the most important gift you can give yourself is the willingness to be wrong. Focus on the process. That's the best way to learn how to be psychic!

You make mistakes.
You learn from your mistakes.
That's how you become the best person you can be!

卌 卌 卌 卌 |||

Recording Sheet for Playing Card Exercise (page 35). Place a tick mark by the "clair" you think you used and by the list of what's going on in your mind.

Clairvoyance (seeing)	**Clairaudience** (hearing/thought)	**Claircognizance** (immediate knowing)	**Clairsentience** (emotion/energy sensing)
卌 ///	卌 ///	卌 ///	卌 ///

Is your mind quiet?

卌 ///　　**YES**　　卌 ///　　**NO**

Thoughts While Playing Psychically With Cards:

Am I getting it right? ✎ 卌 ///...

I'm feeling anxiety in my body. ✎ ....

I used my "trying brain." ✎ ....

I'm getting frustrated. ✎ ....

Are other people doing better than me? ✎ ....

I'm not sure what "clair" I'm using. ✎ ....

I'm not any good at this! ✎ ....

I want to peek. ✎ ....

Other thoughts:

_____
_____
_____
_____
_____
_____
_____

3 A New Way to Learn

When we were kids, we were expected to put forth effort and work hard in school. We were taught thinking and analytical skills, like comparing and contrasting information, so we could better understand something. If we couldn't figure it out, we were told to try harder, to think and analyze, and then to work at it again. That's the "trying brain." For psychic development, you will need a completely different approach. Trying and working hard, so you can "get it," doesn't work with the psychic sense. Yes, practice helps just like it did in school, but working at it—straining, being hard on yourself—just gets in your way.

Psychic learning requires you to get yourself into a space of allowing—the opposite of trying hard. Psychic information comes to you, so you can't go and look for it like you were taught in school. **To be more psychic, you will need to allow something to shift inside of you.** Reading the colors of the playing cards can help you make that shift.

Approaches to Learning

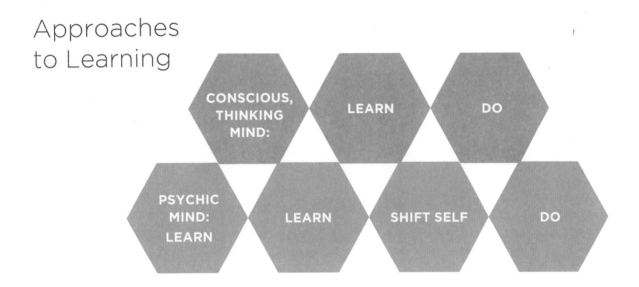

Following are four tips for shifting into this new learning style:

1. Receive instead of reach out for insights.
Psychic information comes towards you, so don't try to look for it; that's your conscious mind. Take on an allowing, receptive frame of mind. Relax by opening your jaw at the hinge; feel your shoulders come down; take in a deep breath and let it out with an audible sigh. Then imagine insights coming towards you like a gentle breeze. It's that same space you were in when you wrote the story "Once upon a time, on a dark and stormy night…"

2. Acknowledge what you get psychically.
When doing psychic work, acknowledge what you get, even if you are doubtful. If you are doing a reading, **tell the person everything you get**—even if you don't understand the significance of it or it seems off-base or bizarre. Just be sensitive to the person, sharing the information in an appropriate way. Acknowledging everything you get sends the message to the psychic part of your mind that you are serious about developing this ability, that you value it, and that you are willing to listen and consider its insights. After all, we have spent most of our lives discounting or ignoring this part of ourselves, and we need to exercise this weak "muscle" by saying everything we get.

In the beginning, you will find that you may get a small piece of information, but not the whole understanding. At these times, you have to speak what little you get. Set aside the conscious mind's desire to know everything before you speak. With practice, you will learn to stay in that connected, psychic space, and a flow of insights will likely come to you after you say just one word.

A woman came to our psychic circle to get a reading from our group. As usual, we entered into meditation. The lights were low. We regularly had visitors, so we could psychically read people we didn't know. We would just speak out what we got. That night, I immediately got information about Sharon.

But I was afraid to speak up. I got that Sharon was concerned she was being abducted by UFO aliens. My first reaction to this was that I had to be wrong—it was weird. And if I was wrong, if that wasn't the reason she came for a reading, then she might think she was being visited by aliens! People seem to think psychics have access to a special source of "truth," and some give psychics far more credence than they should. It's your life. Sure, I'll give you some insights to consider, but ultimately my client is responsible for her own life.

I was too scared to tell Sharon what I got. So like the others, I said that I didn't know why she came for a reading and would she ask her question. Guess what she wanted to know?

Sharon thought she was being abducted by aliens! Ugh! I'd lost the opportunity to value my psychic ability because I'd been afraid of being wrong and looking silly. I learned from that experience.

No matter how difficult it is to tell someone what you are getting (when they ask for a reading), you have to do it. You have to convince your psychic mind that you are serious about valuing it. So you have to say what you get and risk being wrong.

Get over it! You will be wrong in the beginning—perhaps more often than not. But you'll get better, if you have the guts to make the mistakes and then learn from them!

3. Use one of the three "Gs" when you get frustrated or stuck.

One way to successfully improve your psychic skills is to develop strategies to get through this frustration. Let go of the idea that once you develop your psychic muscle, you won't experience being stuck. It will lessen, but you will likely always have some experience of blocked psychic abilities—you are human! The three "Gs" are:

A. GIVE UP. That's what innovators, scientists, business professionals, and creative people do. When they recount how they came to be successful in their endeavor, they often talk about how they worked and worked, but couldn't get it, so they gave up. They let go of trying. And in that open (psychic, imaginative) space, they got an idea that enabled their work to progress.

B. GET PLAYFUL AND PRETEND. When you are stuck, tell a joke to lighten the air or try pretending. If you are doing a reading, pretend you are a great nineteenth-century psychic, dressed like a gypsy with a crystal ball in your third-eye. Peer into your third-eye crystal ball, knowing you will see information to give to your client. Create your own pretend psychic! Try going through your day and playing with being a psychic. This isn't about self-delusion; it's about playacting to get past excessive self-doubt. It's how children learn.

C. GET PISSED! If the other two "Gs" don't work, try getting angry. This won't work if you do it all the time, because getting angry then becomes normal. Has your desk ever been filled with papers and other junk, and you just wanted to shove all that stuff off into a trash can? Well, that's what it's like when you occasionally get pissed! It clears the energetic space so insights can more easily flow to you. Do this silently, saying to yourself something like, "Damn it, give me something now!"

(D. THERE IS A BIGGER, MORE IMPORTANT "G" MAKING FOUR "GS"! But that one needs to be saved until Chapter Five.)

4. Don't use your conscious, thinking mind as a crutch.

When you get something psychically, *go back to what you got*, stay in the psychic space, and ask questions instead of assuming you know the meaning or significance of an image, word, or other insight you get psychically. When we were kids, we learned that when we got a piece of information, we put it into our thinking, analytical mind and processed it to get more information. That's interference in psychic work. When you get a psychic insight and then interpret its meaning with your conscious, thinking mind, you just weakened and devalued your psychic sense.

To be clear, when I say go back to what you got and ask questions—you are asking the questions of the image, thought, feeling, or whatever you got psychically. You are *going back to the psychic source—the energy of it—and **asking the image,** thought, or feeling further questions* and expecting to get more psychic insights.

When you get psychic images, words, feelings, thoughts, or colors, don't assume you know what they mean. Put yourself back into that psychic zone where you got the insight, and be present there as you ask "it" questions, so you can receive additional clarification from a psychic source. Every time you go back and ask more questions psychically, instead of using your conscious mind to interpret it, your psychic abilities get stronger. There will come a day when this process goes faster, and you won't have to keep going back to the psychic source to ask it more questions. The flow of psychic information will happen more readily because you've strengthened your psychic sense, while setting your conscious, thinking mind aside.

Describe what you are getting instead of using a dictionary of symbols. It might be helpful when communicating with spirits to use shorthand, for example, when you see a pink rose, that may mean love is being sent. Although this may be handy at times, it also might hinder giving a more in-depth psychic reading. If you decide to develop a dictionary of symbols, be sure to go beyond that symbol—just as in dreamwork, symbols might have a different significance depending upon who you are reading.

I liken using a dictionary of psychic symbols to weight training. My personal trainer told me that using the machines to lift weights would build muscles, but not as much as using free weights. Yes, the machine (the psychic symbol dictionary) gives you a way to work your muscles. But ask any personal trainer, and you will find that using free weights does a better job of defining and strengthening your muscles. It's the same for the psychic "muscle."

So, when you get an image, word, or other psychic insight, direct questions at what you are sensing, instead of going into your conscious, thinking mind and giving your opinion about it. Put your energy with what you are psychically getting, and then ask a question. For example, ask a color: "What are you about?" This might be slower at first than using a dictionary of symbols, but in the end your psychic muscle will be stronger. The reason I am saying this over and over is so that you get my point: Set aside your conscious, thinking mind and use your psychic sense only when doing psychic work. We are so accustomed to processing information with our thinking mind, that we let it get in the way of building strong psychic abilities.

Dreamwork

Select one word or image from a dream—one that seems significant.

Carry it around in your head as you go through your day.

When you get insights, make notes to put in your journal.

4 What a Healthy Psychic Sense Looks Like

What are you hoping to gain by developing your psychic abilities? This is a good time to reflect on just what you want to get from this workbook. When I ask students what they are striving for, what a healthy psychic sense looks like, they are initially unsure. Below is a list that students have given in the past with some additions. Note the ones that you resonate with and also add to the list.

To be able to access my psychic abilities at will.

To get psychic information quickly.

To receive quality insights that are helpful.

To be in control of my psychic ability, a.k.a. being able to turn it on and off at will.

To trust my psychic abilities.

To be able to listen and be open and ready to receive insights.

To tune in psychically so that distractions (e.g. noise) doesn't bother me.

To get out of my own way.

To know that what I am getting is coming from a psychic source.

To know when I am grounded.

To be able to set my filter aside.

To see to it that my "package" is strong and healthy.

IS IT PSYCHIC?

How do you know that what you are getting is psychic?

It comes when you are in a connected zone that is similar to meditation and the runner's high.

It comes *to* you instead of coming from fantasy, desire, or thinking.

Experience. The more you strengthen your psychic sense, the better you can know when the information you are getting is psychic.

5 How to Evaluate Psychic Information

Just because information comes from a psychic source doesn't make it necessarily right or helpful to you. Images and thoughts can pop into the mind that will not be psychic. Just as your analytical thinking can be wrong or unhelpful, so can psychic information. Use your logical, analytical mind to assess the value of psychic insights, whether they are from a professional psychic or your own psychic sense. Over time, you will develop skills to better determine the accuracy and helpfulness of psychic information. Here are some guidelines to get you started:

1. **Is the psychic information specific?**
   It's nice to get general, supportive encouragement. But psychic information should also provide you with specific, usable information.

2. **Does the psychic information offer new insights?**
   One of the best ways to know you are getting psychic information is whether it is something you hadn't already thought of. Psychic insights should bring out issues and information that you hadn't considered.

3. **Does the psychic information "feel" right?**

Information that feels negative, admonishes or criticizes you, or leaves you without options or hope is not information from a source you want to listen to. Psychic information should leave you inspired and hopeful, even when it challenges you to deal with what you are avoiding and encourages you to grow. It does not suggest you harm someone else or yourself. Psychic information should not be confused with psychosis. Your rational, logical mind is vital for living your life and making good decisions. When in doubt about psychic information, seek advice from trusted friends, family members, and advisors.

4. **Looking back, was the psychic information helpful?**

When you are using your psychic sense to get answers to your questions, keep a record of what you got. Review it periodically to get a sense of how the information benefited you.

KNOW YOURSELF

You can take your psychic abilities further than any program, teacher, or book, if you keep reflecting on how you use your abilities and are willing to examine yourself.

Self-introspection is a key factor in psychic development. Your willingness to look within and examine how your particular psychic sense functions will strengthen your abilities. Use one or more of the following to reflect on how your psychic sense operates as you move through the workbook:

1. Keep a journal about your experiences with your psychic abilities.

2. Create a psychic support group to share your experiences with psychic development.

3. Keep educating yourself, including psychic development, bodywork, meditation, retreats, and continuing education on a variety of subjects. Learn from different teachers—it's good to be exposed to different opinions about things psychic. The curious mind is most psychic.

4. Get a psychic reading on your psychic abilities from a professional psychic, even if you don't want to be a professional psychic.

5. After doing psychic readings or personal psychic work, reflect on how your abilities function using the following questions as a guide:

   - Which "clair" am I using the most?

   - Which is my weakest "clair"?

   - Periodically, intend to use a particular psychic ability or "clair" for that day (or week).

   - Am I asking a person too many questions when I do a reading?

   - What can I learn from my experiences with conducting psychic readings or exercises?

   - How is my body feeling before, during, and after a reading or exercise? Does my body feel drained? Why is this happening? What can I do about it?

   - What affects my psychic abilities? How does my diet affect my psychic sense? How are relationship dynamics affecting my psychic sense? How does my workload affect my psychic sense?

   - Why am I doing psychic work, either professionally or personally?

When you are actively reflective about your inner, psychological world and about your psychic abilities, your readings will have greater depth and complexity. You will give full-bodied readings, instead of superficial, feel-good readings.

NOTES

CHAPTER 3

Meet the "Clairs"
Components of Your Psychic Sense

Officer Pat O'Brien sees a car drifting back and forth across the westbound lanes of Colfax Avenue. Figuring this is a typical drunk driver, O'Brien flips on the flashing lights. But the driver keeps going another two blocks and makes a left turn onto a side street, finally stopping mid-block where it is darkest.

Notifying dispatch, O'Brien angles the car leftward for protection, focusing the high beams and takedown lights on the car ahead. It is a hot summer night, still up in the eighties, even though it is approaching midnight.

O'Brien gets out of the police car and begins the approach. Suddenly, the driver gets out and walks swiftly back toward the officer.

"Stop!" O'Brien yells.

But the driver keeps coming. O'Brien is hit with a rolling wave of cold that seems to envelop the street—a cold so icy that goose bumps instantly rise on her arms. O'Brien intuitively knows this man is extremely dangerous and will do her harm, if she gives him any opportunity.

"Stop! Get back in your car!" Pat yells to the man coming towards her.

Pat gets into her patrol car and backs it up, matching the man's speed coming toward her. The man stops. Quickly radioing for a backup officer, Pat gets out of her patrol car and orders the man back to his car again. "Turn around and put your hands on the back of the trunk." He does so, reluctantly.

Pat frisks him, thinking all the time that if this man felt he had an opportunity to get her gun away from her, he would.

Soon, Officer Steve arrives and saunters toward them as though going to a church social. Pat snaps an order, "Stay back away from him!" Her backup looks confused, but stays out of the man's reach. It should be clear to anyone that Pat is standing in a defensive posture.

(Back in the days of this incident, computers were not available in police cars.) Pat radios dispatch to find out about any outstanding warrants and a criminal history. The history isn't a typical request, but Pat knows in her gut that this guy is a problem.

Dispatch radios back: No warrants; no history. Pat finds that unbelievable. She had never felt a wall of cold like this (and never will again during her career). She knows something is wrong with this guy. She takes him in for drunk driving.

When Pat arrives at the police station, she goes to the clerk who runs criminal histories and stands there, waiting to see the re-check herself. Up comes a lengthy history, including a murder where he tortured a man for fifteen-plus hours before killing him. Somehow, this guy had managed to get a limited sentence and was in a halfway house for prisoners up for parole. He was AWOL, but no one had called that in.

Officer Pat regularly stops drivers who end up having warrants for their arrest. Dispatchers want to know how she does it. Pat just seems to know when a driver has a warrant or something else is wrong about them. "I'd look at them, and it's like they emit an energy that tells me they are a problem. A good cop, a sensitive cop, can pick it up. A lot of cops do this, but they just don't know they do it."

As they'd driven to the jail, the man had pleaded in a smooth-as-butter voice for Officer Pat to take him back to the halfway house. Deep in her gut, she'd known the guy was a psychopath. Finally realizing that he wouldn't be able to change her mind, he'd snarled and hissed at her. But he quickly recovered his smooth façade and sunnily wished her well.

It's ridiculous that our society makes light of psychic ability. We need these instincts. Most of us won't need them for life-and-death matters like a police officer. But when you develop your natural ability, you will have additional resources for making better life decisions. We are all using our psychic sense anyway, so why not improve our ability to access it.

Without knowing the specific terms for it, Officer Pat had clearly benefited from two aspects of her psychic sense: she had "felt" an icy wave of cold as the murderer had walked back toward her, and she had just "known" that the guy was a dangerous psychopath. Psychic ability is composed of our basic senses accompanied by an expanded awareness—which is the psychic component. We all incorporate some psychic input along with our basic senses, most of us without ever being aware of it.

Perhaps a better term for the psychic sense is *ESP*. That's what we called the psychic sense over forty years ago. Various social scientists and even our own Defense Department researched it. But things psychic were not provable or predictable using reductionist scientific methods. And the term *Extra Sensory Perception*, a term that more accurately reflects how the psychic sense operates, was dropped from the popular lexicon.

A helpful way to understand ESP or the psychic sense is to break it down into its component parts —the "clairs."

Clairsentience
PSYCHIC FEELING (EMOTIONS AND ENERGY)

Clairvoyance
PSYCHIC SEEING

Clairaudience
PSYCHIC HEARING

Claircognizance
PSYCHIC KNOWING

Clairalience
PSYCHIC SMELLING

Clairgustance
PSYCHIC TASTING

Create Your Package!

As I mentioned earlier, the muscles in our body provide a useful model for thinking about all the components of the psychic sense. Just like our physical muscles, we use our psychic "muscles" all the time without thinking about it. Some people want to develop their muscles—psychic and physical. To do so means paying attention to what is normally involuntary.

A body builder uses specific exercises to develop all aspects of a muscle. For example, the deltoid muscle covers the shoulder joint, and it has three distinct parts. Body builders use different exercises to isolate the three parts of this muscle, so the overall muscle can be effectively developed and defined. Psychic development involves a similar approach with the psychic sense.

Just like our physical muscles, there are parts to the psychic "muscle." These parts are the six individual "clairs." There is overlap in using them, but you can still isolate the parts to develop them further. By doing so, your overall psychic sense will become stronger.

Most people primarily use one or two "clairs," for example, clairvoyance (seeing) or clairsentience (feeling emotions or energy). But to develop your psychic sense fully—to make your psychic muscle most effective—set aside your strongest "clairs" and give particular focus to the exercises that will develop your weakest "clairs."

What is your strongest "clair" now? What is your weakest "clair"? As you move through this workbook, continue asking yourself this. Following is a list of my strongest and weakest "clairs." On the page that follows is a place for you to record where you are now in regards to your "clairs." In the past, students who completed this form were surprised at how far they had come when they reviewed the information six months after working on their abilities.

My "Clairs"

1990 WITH 2014 UPDATE FOR KAREN FOX

STRENGTHS	WEAKNESSES
Clairsentience: I just graduated from massage school. My awareness of energy has blossomed. I remember when I couldn't feel energy in my body or in anyone else's. *Update:* I use clairsentience in a healthy way. I hardly ever let other people's emotions and energy get me down, and this used to happen all the time. I was viewed as overly "sensitive" as a child.	**Clairsentience:** My emotions, being empathic, can still overwhelm me and get in the way of my being psychic. I need to work on ways my childhood stuff gets triggered when I psychically connect to people. *Update:* Although I'm pretty body aware, I would like to add energy movement to my daily life, such as Qi Gong. I think this would expand my psychic abilities.
Clairvoyance: Almost from day one of massage school, I started seeing in my mind's eye images that I later learned were connected to the people I was massaging. This and clairsentience are my primary ways of being psychic. *Update:* This is no longer my primary way of being psychic. I use clairvoyance at times to clarify what I'm getting with claircognizance. Sometimes, images come without my intentionally using clairvoyance. It's like clairvoyance is there when I need it, even though I don't use it as much as I once did.	**Clairvoyance:** It takes so much time to figure out what a particular image means. I think I know what the images are telling me, but when I talk with a client, it has a different interpretation. I need to stay out of the way of what I get psychically by not using my thinking to figure out what a clairvoyant image means. And it takes me so much time to use clairvoyance! *Update:* I think I'll spend some time each day developing my clairvoyance. I tend now to use claircognizance almost exclusively. But I wonder what my overall psychic ability would be like if I returned to focusing on specific "clairs"— isolating them again to see if I could expand them even further.
Clairaudience: I started "hearing" psychic insights almost from the time my clairvoyance kicked in. Doing hands-on Reiki sessions every week provides me with the basis for developing clairaudience and clairvoyance. *Update:* I tend to use more clairaudience when my client has these skills. I use my clairaudience more when communicating with spirits than I do when using my psychic abilities in other ways.	**Clairaudience:** I don't hear psychically like I do with my regular hearing. Before I started charging for readings, I frequently got names (& the relevant information). I clearly have a block here. I'm not sure yet why I have this block. *Update:* The block is about my issues with deserving good things in my life. I've been working on this in therapy, and I'm beginning to get names again. Also, I have come to realize that everyone is uniquely psychic, and the way I do clairaudience is acceptable. I "hear" with my inner ears. I don't want to hear psychically like I do with my regular hearing. I have honed my clairaudience so that it doesn't unbalance me because I know where the "hearing" is coming from.

STRENGTHS	WEAKNESSES
Claircognizance: This "clair" seems to be active when I'm in the moment of major crisis. I hardly notice it at other times, or if I'm even using it. *Update:* Claircognizance is my strongest "clair" and all my other "clairs" support this.	**Claircognizance:** I don't have the self-esteem to just say what I immediately get psychically. I let doubt get in my way. *Update:* I trust myself. I hardly ever let doubt get in the way of my psychic readings. I've done hypnotherapy that has helped me move through the anxiety I feel when self-esteem issues get triggered. Immediate knowings are coming to me fairly frequently during the day about my life without my asking, and this is flowing into my readings, where I'm getting clear insights about my clients' possible future.
Clairalience: Psychic smelling comes sometimes without my focusing on it. *Update:* I have tried to develop my psychic smelling, and I have more experiences of it during readings, especially when communicating with spirits.	**Clairalience:** I hardly ever experience psychic smelling. I've never thought of this as being important to my psychic development. *Update:* I'm still pretty lazy when it comes to strengthening my psychic smelling.
Clairgustance: What!? I never figured there was such a thing as psychic tasting. I've only had one experience that just came to me during a reading I was giving. *Update:* Pretty much the same.	**Clairgustance:** Clearly my weakest "clair." I need to practice what I teach and strengthen this "clair," so that all my "clairs" can benefit! *Update:* Pretty much the same. I need to get busy using some of my own exercises to get better at this.

My "Clairs"

STRENGTHS	WEAKNESSES
Clairsentience:	**Clairsentience:**
Clairvoyance:	**Clairvoyance:**
Clairaudience:	**Clairaudience:**

STRENGTHS	WEAKNESSES
Claircognizance:	**Claircognizance:**
Clairalience:	**Clairalience:**
Clairgustance:	**Clairgustance:**

Dreamwork

Select one of your dreams.

Get watercolors, crayons, colored pencils, paper, or other art material.

Paint or color something about a dream, like an abstract picture of how your dream makes you feel or a more detailed drawing of a specific part of your dream.

Put the date of the dream on the back of your image.

Paint something about your dreams on a regular basis. Later in the workbook, you will be given instructions on what to do with your pictures. For now, just paint or color your dreams. You will need at least ten pictures. You will see "Dreamwork" boxes throughout the workbook, reminding you to paint 10+ pictures of your dreams.

EACH OF THE FOLLOWING SECTIONS IS FOR ONE SPECIFIC "CLAIR."

If another "clair" comes up when you are doing the exercises, set it aside, and return your focus to the "clair" you are learning about.

1 Clairsentience

(PSYCHIC FEELING & ENERGY SENSING)

> Snooty the manatee was swimming around in a much-too-small tank at a marine center in Bradenton, Florida. I had just moved from the Washington, D.C., area, and I wanted to see what a manatee looked like up close. Snooty was playful, swimming around, splashing water on all of us lined up around his open tank.
>
> I wanted Snooty to come near me. So I sent my energy awareness out from my hands to him. He immediately zipped over to where I was standing and leapt onto the side of the tank. I took a step backward, wanting to hug him, but not wanting to harm Snooty. We had been asked not to get our germs on him. I was thrilled! People screamed with excitement.
>
> Fortunately, today, Snooty has a much bigger living environment, and it is closed off, so no one can touch him.

Definition: (French. *clair*=clear and *sentience*=feeling)

Clairsentience refers to the ability to get information through feeling psychically, which includes both sensing feelings/emotions and energy. Typically thought of as having to do with picking up on other people's emotions, a particularly clairsentient person is called an "empath." Women are thought of as being naturally empathic. Although this may have some basis in our biology, we encourage (and allow) females to emote. Boys are still getting the message that it is not okay to express feelings.

Clairsentience is also involved in touch. Psychometry is related to clairsentience in that psychic information is gained by holding an object and feeling its energy. Energy workers are using clairsentience, particularly when they sense the energy and vibrations in a client's body.

I was reminded of clairsentience when I saw a video on the news of a young girl at an aquatic center standing in front of a large, floor-to-ceiling tank with a seal. As the girl danced along the length of the tank, the seal simultaneously matched her movements. They danced in unison, making the same movements at the same time. The seal abruptly stopped when the child stopped. This normal connection between species occurs through clairsentience—the dance of energy that connects us all.

Even the biggest skeptic of psychic abilities has most likely had the experience of entering a room and having an immediate sense of the energy in that room or of the group that has gathered there. That's clairsentience operating, and we human animals, just like other animals, come by this ability naturally.

Exercises to Increase Clairsentience:

SENSING ENERGY IN YOUR HANDS

Relax jaw, take a breath, connect with your body; are you relaxed?

Everyone has healing energy in their hands to some extent. And you don't have to take a class in massage or energywork to connect with and use this energy. This exercise will increase your psychic sense by increasing your body awareness.

Rub your hands/palms together several times. Then hold your palms facing each other about one to three inches apart. What do you feel between your hands? Lightly pump the energy in the space between the palms (without touching the palms) by slowly moving your palms towards each other and then slightly away from each other. What do you sense?

Put your hands on your body. Move your hands to an area of your body that is hurting or uncomfortable. Keep your fingers and thumb together—this intensifies the energy flowing through your palms. Imagine a beautiful color flowing through your hands and into your body where it hurts. Keep your awareness deep in the area you are touching, and be open to sensing shifts in the texture, movement, and color of the energy.

Disconnect when you are finished. You will usually know when giving yourself healing energy feels complete. Or you can just decide that you are finished. Disengage by shaking your hands.

What was your experience?

Exercise to Increase Clairsentience:

SENDING/SENSING EMOTIONS

Relax jaw, take a breath, connect with your body; are you relaxed?

Pair up. Sit close to each other, about one to two feet away. Send a strong emotion to your partner, like anger or love. Try visualizing an experience when you had this emotion and send that experience to your partner.

For individuals: Do this exercise with a pet. Animals (and young children) more easily sense and react to energy or the thoughts in the room. How does the pet/child react? Disconnect by getting up and going outside to sit on the ground, or wash your hands.

What was your experience?

Cautions about Clairsentience:

The risk of using clairsentience or empathic ways of being psychic is that you can become enmeshed with people and pickup their emotions and physical ailments. Clairsentience requires strong, healthy psychological boundaries and the ability to be aware when your boundaries are being violated and when you are crossing others' boundaries. You will need to learn how to disengage from your connection with their emotions and energy so you don't carry their stuff with you.

Of prime importance is to be able to stay within your own body and psyche while you use your psychic abilities, so that you don't collapse in a pool of emotions or body aches. If you want to be a professional psychic and you are crying along with your clients or feeling their physical issues in your body on a regular basis, you have crossed a boundary between you and another person. You will not be able to effectively assist others if you are processing their stuff inside you. You are human, so a feeling response is normal and makes you compassionate—it is a matter of degree.

I have found that when I've overly connected with my psychic reading clients (and when I did hands-on energywork) using clairsentience, my body weight increased. My weight became a boundary for me, because I was not able to create that boundary in my own psyche. It's for this reason that, early in my work as a professional psychic, I chose to mostly set aside a clairsentient way of being psychic. In the process, I discovered that my other ways of being psychic got stronger. And now when I use clairsentience in a reading, I don't usually have emotional reactions. Nor do I have overwhelming physical sensations when I walk into a room with difficult energy. I'm also not afraid of spirits or so-called hauntings. This came from doing inner psychological work, bodywork, and setting aside (for a time) clairsentient ways of being psychic.

SIGNS THAT YOUR CLAIRSENTIENCE NEEDS BETTER BOUNDARIES:

1. You feel like the emotions of others are yours, you take responsibility for their emotions, and/or you are overly affected by others' emotions.

2. You are fatigued and drained after being around people or when doing psychic work.

3. You eat more when around demanding people.

4. You give and give and then give some more, and you don't give enough to yourself. Families and certain jobs can sometimes require more giving (as in end-of-life care of a family member). But if you prefer the giving role and you can't give to yourself, then you will likely have difficulty doing psychic work. Do your inner work and create healthy boundaries.

Using clairsentience is something for you to decide whether or not to use. I understand why you might want to rely on clairsentience—it is likely the most natural, easy way many of us function psychically in our lives. But focusing on clairsentience solely is like developing your right arm muscles and leaving your left arm muscles flabby.

Exercise to Increase Clairsentience:

BODY AWARENESS—WHERE YOUR BOUNDARIES BEGIN AND END

Close your eyes. Sense your body; relax your jaw. Observe your breath for a couple minutes. Extend your energy awareness into the field of energy around your body. Be with this energy for a few moments.

Then put your hand over your solar plexus just above your belly button. What happens to your energy?

As you go through the day, pause to become aware of where your energy is. It might be out in the room somewhere, with another person, or more likely, you don't know where it is. After finding your energy, put your hand on your solar plexus. Your energy will likely return to you, and you will be aware of it inside your body. This exercise will increase your body awareness, and body awareness is psychic awareness.

What was your experience?

_____
_____
_____
_____
_____
_____
_____
_____
_____
_____
_____
_____
_____
_____
_____
_____
_____
_____
_____
_____
_____
_____
_____
_____
_____
_____

Create Your Package!

TIP FOR GOOD BOUNDARIES:

How is your body feeling now?

Shake your hands. Expand the shaking to include your arms and lastly your whole body. Relax.

How is your body feeling now?

Answers to Your Question

Below is a technique to psychically read a question about your life. (More techniques will follow.) Write a clear, brief question that you will use throughout this workbook. Use this same question for all the psychic readings you will be doing under the headings, "Answers to Your Question." At the end of Chapter 4, you will evaluate all the information you have gained using these reading techniques. So don't keep changing your question.

Examples of questions: What is the best career for me? How can I improve my financial situation? How can I find the best life partner for me? What can I do about my relationship problems with (name)? When is a good time for me to move? What is important for me to know about my life now?

My Question:

_____

_____

_____

_____

_____

_____

_____

_____

_____

_____

_____

_____

_____

_____

_____

_____

_____

_____

READ USING CLAIRSENTIENCE:

Relax jaw, take a breath, and connect with your body. With your intention, send your energy into the field of energy around your body. Be with this energy for a few moments.

Then send your energy further into the room and be present with the room for a moment. Pull it back into your body by placing your hand over your solar plexus.

Now send your energy to your question. Be inside the energy of the question, so you are one with the question. Ask the question and expect to receive insights.

If this seems weird, or you don't know what to do, pretend. Read through the instructions and pretend to do them. With practice, you will come to understand how to do this. This technique can be used to make a connection to whatever you want to read: a person, a question, a time in the future, and more.

When you are finished, disconnect by placing your hand on your solar plexus, and feel your energy return to you.

Record insights in your journal. Use your analytical mind to assess the insights. What steps might you take in your life based on what you got psychically? When you value your psychic insights by using them, your psychic sense gets stronger.

HOW TO *NOT* TO PICK UP SOMEONE ELSE'S "STUFF":

1. **Do your inner work.** Psychotherapy, hypnotherapy, retreats, bodywork, dream groups—any small group focused on personal growth, or any method that helps you do your inner, psychological work. Smudging, affirmations, bubbles around your body, or anything of that ilk can be helpful—but nothing beats having good psychological health and boundaries.

2. **Establish a regular ritual to disconnect after psychic work.** You might also use the same ritual before starting psychic work. Doing the same thing over and over cements in your mind and body that you are grounded and centered; that you know yourself and your abilities; and that you are empowered to help, but not be drained by your helping. It doesn't matter so much what the ritual is—create what you like and do it regularly so that it becomes rote memory in the cells of your being. I wash my hands. Others say a prayer. Do what you prefer.

3. **Learn to ground and disconnect.** There is plenty of material available with suggestions for how to shield yourself and cleanse your energy field. The next paragraph provides some beginning ideas. I will cover this further in Chapter Five.

WHAT TO DO WHEN YOU HAVE PICKED UP SOMEONE ELSE'S STUFF:

The following is helpful for doing any psychic work, particularly when using clairsentience.

*   Wash your hands. It's amazing what this simple task can do for disconnecting from someone's energy.

*   Put your hand on your solar plexus. Affirm, "My energy is with me. Your energy is with you."

*   Shake your hands, and let the shaking move up your arms into your whole body until your whole body is dancing off the stuff.

*   Smile. Laugh—laughter is always the best medicine.

*   Be careful what you eat, so that you don't "process" what you've picked up by eating. Figure out what foods help you to ground yourself without sending you into compulsive eating.

*   Do something physical—walk, run, dance, do jumping jacks.

*   Get into the green zone—being in Nature is curative and calming. Try putting your feet in a pond or creek.

*   What is it that you have picked up? Being aware of that is part of letting it go.

Dreamwork

Remember to paint your dreams

Get watercolors, crayons, colored pencils, paper, or other art material.

Paint or color something about a dream, like an abstract picture of how your dream makes you feel or a more detailed drawing of a specific part of your dream.

Put the date of the dream on the back.

Paint something about your dreams on a regular basis. Later in the workbook, you will be given instructions on what to do with your pictures. For now, just paint or color your dreams. You will need at least ten pictures.

2 Clairvoyance
(PSYCHIC SEEING)

Lisa was five years old, and her dog had just died. She walked out on her porch, and to her surprise, she saw a little, white, fluffy-haired dog. Lisa played all day with it and later went inside to ask her mother if she could keep it. Her Mom said, "Yes." Thirty years later, Lisa's mother told her that she had never seen the dog. What a wonderfully affirming Mom!

Lisa regularly talked with two friends that only *she* could see—Mimi and Sa Sa Bonnett, sisters from France. After a time, her mother became concerned that Lisa seemed to be too focused on what wasn't "real," so she took her to the doctor. Fortunately, the doctor said it was normal for little Lisa to play with "imaginary friends" who weren't so imaginary to Lisa. She saw the sisters with her naked eyes, just like she had seen the dog years before.

At 16, Lisa wasn't seeing spirits anymore, or so she thought. When her family moved into a new house, she plopped down on a sofa for a rest after moving boxes. As clear as day, a Native American walked diagonally across the room. She was totally freaked this time. Older then, she didn't see such things anymore—nor was it acceptable in her everyday world. After that, she felt his presence, but no longer saw him. Lisa sculptured a bust of him that sits in her home still.

As an adult, Lisa uses clairvoyance in her work as a psychic aura painter, but she mostly sees with her inner, psychic eye. She did have occasion to see a man one day when she was walking in Crown Hill Park near a cemetery. It had been a difficult day and Lisa was in a bad mood. She had just turned the corner where she could see the cemetery, when a man came towards her. As he approached Lisa, he held out his hand and greeted her, "Isn't it a beautiful day!" They shook hands, and he was as solid as anyone.

Immediately, Lisa's mood lifted, but as she turned around to see him one last time, he wasn't there. The man *should* have been there, but he wasn't. After thinking about it, she realized everything about the man was out-of-place for her time period. He had been wearing a 1940s tweed, three-piece suit and a coat and hat—something men didn't wear in her time, and it wasn't cold enough to dress so heavily. But it didn't matter, because she felt wonderful for the rest of the day. Something about his greeting had touched her in a special way.

Definition: (French. *clair*=clear and *voyance*=vision)

Clairvoyance refers to the ability to be able to obtain information by seeing psychically. In my experience, this is the way most people receive psychic information (after clairsentience). Some people have difficulty visualizing, and this can get in the way of accessing clairvoyant skills. But like all the "clairs," it can be improved with practice.

Clairvoyance occurs in three ways:

1. Seeing something psychically with the "naked" eyes,

2. Seeing something with the inner eye, or

3. Seeing a flash of something, usually with the "naked" eye, out of the corner of an eye.

Helen Gilman (1892-1985) was a psychic in Boulder, Colorado. She was nearly blind when she read tea leaves, but despite her handicap (or maybe because of it), Helen clairvoyantly read over 80,000 people in 75 years. People from all walks of life sought her out, including actor Douglas Fairbanks and sororities and fraternities at the University of Colorado at Boulder. (http://www.dailycamera.com/features/ci_13585150)

Remote Viewing, which draws upon clairvoyance skills, was used to gather defense-related information from a distance in a project developed and sponsored by the CIA and the United States Air Force, under the Stargate Project. Soviets had conducted research into the military uses of psychic abilities (see: *Psychic*

Discoveries Behind the Iron Curtain, by Sheila Ostrander and Lynn Schroeder), and the United States military did not want to fall behind. Soldiers were recruited and taught how to Remote View. Some had little or no previous interest or ability in things psychic, but they were successful, and some soldiers turned out to be psychically gifted.

The expectation that to be really psychic you must psychically see with your naked eyes (or hear with your "naked" ears) is a waste of time. First, that's a value common in our Western world that only values what can be seen or touched. Second, just ask any police officer about eyewitness testimony. (It can't be relied upon.) Third, do you really want your life to be interrupted by psychic seeing with your naked eyes?

Lisa and I taught aura painting classes, but neither of us saw auras with our "naked eyes." As we talked about our students' expectations that they should see auras with their naked eyes, we both found out that, as children, we would gaze into the air and see little squiggly lines and dots moving around—much like the contrast on the television when it used to go off air. We can still see these textures in and around objects, places, and people when we relax. I think this way of seeing energy contributed to my ability to do energywork sessions with clients as a medical intuitive. As I scanned the client's body, I could see this kind of textured energy. How you "see" psychically is unique to every person, and you will discover that your clairvoyance changes as you develop your overall psychic abilities. Lisa now sometimes sees auras with her naked eyes, though she thinks this isn't necessary to do psychic work.

Exercise to Increase Clairvoyance:

FOCUS ON WHAT YOU SEE. RELAX JAW, TAKE A BREATH, CONNECT WITH YOUR BODY; ARE YOU RELAXED?

We are always getting psychic input, but we have been taught to ignore it as not valuable or credible. As you go about your day, focus on what you see. This will carry over to your psychic sense. Here are some suggestions:

- Pause at times, and see yourself seeing, as if you are observing yourself watching.
- Sense colors more fully—pause for a bit longer than typical and put your focus on a color.
- When an image comes to you psychically, pause and pay attention to it—be with it before rushing to figure out what it is communicating.

What was your experience?

Breathe ...

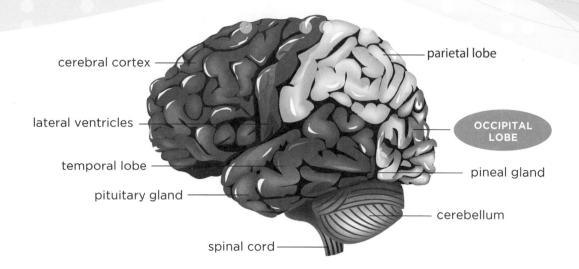

cerebral cortex

parietal lobe

lateral ventricles

OCCIPITAL LOBE

temporal lobe

pineal gland

pituitary gland

cerebellum

spinal cord

Exercise to Increase Clairvoyance:

OCCIPITAL LOBE BREATHING.
USE CLAIRSENTIENCE TO ACTIVATE YOUR CLAIRVOYANCE.

Get in that connected, quiet zone. Try observing your breath to get there. Then put your awareness inside your occipital lobe. Be present there for a moment before continuing with this exercise.

With your intention, breathe with your occipital lobe, as if only this lobe was doing all your breathing. With every inhalation, feel the back of your head expanding. When you exhale, feel the back of your head relax. Imagine you are filling the occipital lobe with fresh energy every time you inhale, releasing whatever needs releasing when you exhale. If you don't feel a movement in the occipital lobe or back of your head, continue practicing this exercise. At some point, you will easily sense your occipital lobe "breathing." Practice occipital lobe breathing for one to two minutes off and on throughout the day/evening.

As with any of these altered state exercises, don't do them when you need to pay attention to what you are doing, like driving a car.

Create Your Package!

TIP TO DISCONNECT:

You need to have clear energy boundaries between you and others to do psychic work. Just noticing when you have picked up someone's energy or when you are still connected to whatever (or whoever) you were psychically reading are good first steps towards establishing healthy energy boundaries.

Close your eyes. Where is your energy? Is someone's energy still with you?

Put your hand on your solar plexus (just above your belly button). Affirm to yourself, "My energy is with me. Your energy is with you."

Where is your energy now?

Exercise to Increase Clairvoyance:

WHAT'S IN THE ENVELOPE?

Clip ten-plus images from magazines and glue or tape them each to a piece of white paper. Put each image into a large, plain envelope so the clipping is not folded. Keep some of the images simple in design, without showing a lot of detail. Include some images with only one or two colors and with only one or two items in the picture.

After some time passes, you will likely not recall the pictures, and then you can use them to do this exercise. Or have a friend put pictures in envelopes for you so that you do not have any awareness of their contents.

Mix up the envelopes, select one envelope, and put the others aside. If you'd like, take the envelope with you as you go about your day. Tune in and make notes as suggested below. You might find it easier to get psychic information when you don't put a lot of effort into getting it.

Be in that connected, quiet zone. Tune in psychically to the picture, and draw what you "see."

Do NOT—*NOT!*— start the exercise by trying to figure out what is in the envelope!

START by drawing the *shapes* and noting the *colors*. Let shapes and colors *come to you*.

ONLY *after* you have drawn the shapes and colors, do you step back from the picture you have drawn to get a broader sense of what is in it.

For two or more individuals: One person will be the sender and the other(s) will be the receiver(s). The sender opens the envelope and focuses on the image, using all the senses to make the image come alive—taste, touch, smell, sight, hearing, emotions. That person should use the mind to send these sensations along with the image to the receiver(s). Pretend you are sending these sensations and the image into the receiver's head. The receiver records what they get about the image by coloring a picture or taking descriptive notes. Then have fun sharing what everyone received.

What was your experience?

_____

_____

_____

_____

_____

_____

_____

_____

_____

_____

_____

_____

_____

_____

_____

Answers to Your Question

READ USING CLAIRVOYANCE

Breathe with your occipital lobe until you feel connected with it. Then go deeper into your occipital lobe and find that "sweet spot" where you feel connected to a psychic kind of seeing (you'll just *know* with practice). Ask the question you have about your life, recorded earlier on page 62. Allow images to come to you.

When you get an image, go back inside the energy of the image, and ask the image for more psychic information. Stay out of your analytical, thinking mind.

When you are finished, disconnect by shutting the door to your third-eye.

Record insights in your journal. Spend some time thinking about the information you received from this exercise. What makes sense to you? What doesn't seem to fit with your typical way of thinking? Making notes about this in your journal strengthens your psychic abilities.

3 Clairaudience

(PSYCHIC HEARING)

Jim had just started to work in downtown Washington, D.C., for the United States Treasury Department. A math guy, he was overwhelmed with all the new assignments and always seemed to be preoccupied. He often went for a walk at lunchtime to take in the sights.

All the traffic lights at an intersection in D.C. turn red, so pedestrians can then cross in any direction, even diagonally across the intersection. Jim was just ready to cross an intersection, about a block from the White House. As he stepped off the curb, head bent downward and totally focused on thinking about his new job, he immediately saw in his peripheral vision a blurry image of a person form to his left and somewhat elevated. The man screamed, "Stop, watch out!" Jim stopped and looked up just as a car running the red light came racing through the intersection at a high rate of speed. It missed Jim by inches.

Jim looked again to his left, but the man who had screamed was gone. There was no one in sight. To this day, Jim isn't sure what happened, but his inner voice told him this was out of the realm of the ordinary. Even though the image of the person was blurry, Jim could tell it had been a man looking directly at him. Jim wonders if it was a spirit or guardian angel—if there were such things.

Definition: (French. *clair*=clear and *audience*=hearing)

Clairaudience refers to the ability to get information by hearing psychically. Clairaudient hearing of words, music, and other sounds can occur in three ways:

1. The sound is actually heard in a person's head,

2. The sound is actually heard out loud in the room, and

3. A thought or idea is impressed on your mind, usually in a quick flash.

Claircognizance can overlap with clairaudience—all the "clairs" overlap at some level. Some view getting a thought as the same as claircognizance. But, typically, claircognizance comes as a direct knowing, without specific words or thoughts—you just know.

Clairaudience is not schizophrenia. Some students and parents of psychic children have expressed concern about their hearing things—afraid this might indicate mental health problems. Schizophrenia isn't just about hearing things or thoughts in the head. This mental disorder involves getting directions that are not in the best interest of the person receiving them and can be detrimental to others. Check with a mental health professional if this concerns you.

Psychic hearing can cause anxiety, particularly in childhood, when sensing spirits. TV programs and movies add to fear of the spirit world because of the scary nature of some of the storylines. It might be helpful to know that what is often portrayed on television or in the theater does not reflect the way spirit communication happens. If you are feeling fear or anxiety about hearing spirits, do some inner work to discover what might be triggering this fear in you. This can get you past anxieties and fears about psychic hearing and spirit communication.

> If you are afraid of your psychic awareness, your imagination will conjure up all sorts of horrid things.— Cassandra Eason
>
> *Psychic Power of Children* (p. 142)

When I first started developing my abilities, I rarely got full, complete sentences or thoughts with clairaudience. The conscious, thinking mind wants the complete understanding. If you always tell a person you are reading whatever you get, even if it is one or two words—more will usually come. Resist trying to interpret psychic hearing with your conscious mind. Say what you get, and then go back to what you got with your psychic hearing for more insights. This will strengthen your clairaudience.

In 1990, when I started giving readings, I asked a professional psychic medium how she got names during a reading. She replied, "Just decide you're going to do it." That seemed too simplistic to actually work. But I made the decision that the next time I did a reading, I would get a name and relevant descriptive information.

About a week later, I was reading someone I had never met, and during the session, I gave her a name and told her that she was going to do dance work with this person. She had a perplexed look on her face as she searched for that name and description in her memory, but couldn't find it. I was doing practice readings at the time, so we just chalked it up to a miss. But when she was getting ready to leave and looking through her purse for her keys, a shocked look came on her face. She pulled out a small piece of paper with the name on it that I had given her. She told me that she had just met this person, and maybe that's why she didn't recall her name. The woman she had met was a dance instructor whom she'd wanted to learn from!

So if you think you can't get clairaudient information, just decide that you can!

Exercise to Increase Clairaudience:

FOCUS ON WHAT YOU HEAR.

As you go about your day, focus on what you hear. This will carry over to your psychic sense. Here are some suggestions:

Pause at times, and focus on your hearing. Pay special attention to the quality of someone's voice and sound.

Sense hearing more fully. Sense the subtle sounds that are around you all the time—the birds singing, that noise in the hallway.

What was your experience?

_____

_____

_____

_____

_____

_____

_____

_____

_____

_____

_____

_____

_____

Breathe ...

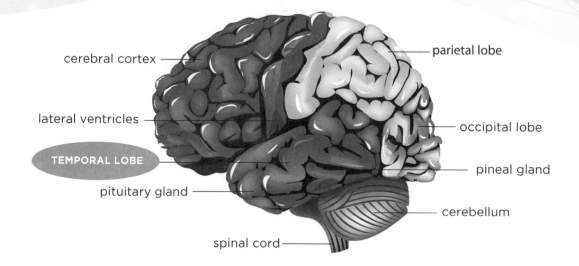

cerebral cortex

lateral ventricles

TEMPORAL LOBE

pituitary gland

spinal cord

parietal lobe

occipital lobe

pineal gland

cerebellum

Exercise to Increase Clairaudience:

TEMPORAL LOBE BREATHING.
USE CLAIRSENTIENCE TO ACTIVATE YOUR CLAIRAUDIENCE.

Get in that connected, quiet zone. Put your awareness inside your temporal lobes. Be present there for a moment before continuing with this exercise.

With your intention, breathe with the temporal lobe structures as if only these lobes were doing your breathing. You might play with breathing with just one temporal lobe at a time and note the difference, if any, on the two sides.

With every inhalation, feel the space above your ears expanding. When you exhale, feel this area relax. Imagine you are filling your temporal lobes with fresh energy every time you inhale, releasing whatever needs releasing when you exhale. If you don't feel a movement in the temporal lobes, continue practicing this exercise. At some point you will easily sense your temporal lobes "breathing." Practice temporal lobe breathing for one to two minutes off and on throughout the day/evening.

As with any of these altered-state exercises, don't do them when you have to pay attention to what you are doing, like driving a car.

Exercise to Increase Clairaudience:

Get a friend to send you a word or brief message throughout the day. Go about your day expecting that you will get the message by "hearing" it psychically. Feel deep in your gut that your friend's message is coming to you clearly. When doubt about this comes up, laugh at it.

Talk later in the evening to discuss what you got and what your friend sent. Don't be self-critical if you didn't get the message—chuckle about it, even if you are upset that you didn't get it.

What was your experience?

_____
_____
_____
_____
_____

Create Your Package!

TIP TO GROUNDING:

Imagine you are an ancient oak tree, and you can feel your roots going deep into the ground.

Even better, go outside and hug a tree, or sit at the base of one and lean against it. Feel the tree's energy, and take your energy down the tree into its roots going deep inside the ground.

Exercise to Increase Clairaudience:

COLOR OF CARDS

Relax jaw, take a breath, connect with your body; are you relaxed?

Pair up and clairaudiently read the color of the suit of a regular deck of playing cards. Focus on "hearing" the color (red or black) psychically instead of using the other "clairs." You might try placing your awareness inside your temporal lobes to assist you.

The person holding the card can send the color to the reader to assist—say the color silently to yourself, so your partner can better "hear" the color. To reduce performance anxiety, I recommend you wait until the end of the deck to see how you did.

For individuals: Place the 10 of Hearts and a 10 of Clubs face up. Select one card at a time and expect to psychically hear the color (red or black). Place the card with the appropriate 10 of Hearts/red or Clubs/black.

What was your experience?

Dreamwork

Remember to paint your dreams

Get watercolors, crayons, colored pencils, paper, or other art material.

Paint or color something about a dream, like an abstract picture of how your dream makes you feel or a more detailed drawing of a specific part of your dream.

Put the date of the dream on the back.

Paint something about your dreams on a regular basis. Later in the workbook, you will be given instructions on what to do with your pictures. For now, just paint or color your dreams. You will need at least ten pictures.

Exercise to Increase Clairaudience:

YES/NO QUESTIONS

Relax jaw, take a breath, connect with your body; are you relaxed?

Pair up. One partner asks the following questions.

The reader expects to hear "Yes" or "No" in response to the questions. Do not get any more information. Focus your psychic sense JUST on hearing "Yes" or "No."

- Have I ever been in California?

- Do I have a dog now?

- Is my grandmother on my mother's side still living?

- Is my car blue?

A married couple in my mentor group decided to keep a bowl of questions with obvious yes/no answers on the kitchen counter, so that when they passed by the bowl, they would do this exercise. They more regularly exercised their psychic skills by having this handy.

For individuals: Put each of the above questions on separate pieces of paper and place inside envelopes. Mix, and select an envelope to read. Record the answer you "hear" on the envelope. After you read all the questions in the envelopes, open them to see how you did.

What was your experience?

_____

_____

_____

_____

_____

_____

_____

_____

_____

_____

_____

_____

_____

_____

_____

_____

_____

_____
_____
_____
_____
_____
_____
_____
_____
_____
_____
_____
_____
_____
_____
_____
_____
_____
_____
_____
_____

Answers to Your Question

READ USING CLAIRAUDIENCE

Pair up. Do temporal lobe breathing to engage your clairaudience.

One person should psychically read the question below while holding the expectation that you will "hear" a song in response.

Tell your partner what song you hear. Then discuss the significance. Do an Internet search for the complete lyrics by typing the lyrics you do know, along with the word "lyrics," in the search engine, and you will likely pull up the song.

WHAT'S GETTING IN MY WAY?

For individuals: Write three questions about your life that you would like insights about. For example: What's getting in my way? What do I need to know about my job? How is my health? Put your questions on separate pieces of paper and put in separate envelopes. Mix, and select an envelope to read. Do temporal lobe breathing to engage your clairaudience. Expect to "hear" a song that will give you insights into the question in the envelope. Make a note of the song on the envelope. After you have gotten songs for all the envelopes, open them to get your insights. Do an Internet search for the complete lyrics.

Record insights in your journal. Make note of the lyrics in your journal. What do you think the lyrics are telling you about your question? If possible, locate a recording of the song, and play it while you write about how the song connects to your question.

4 Claircognizance

(PSYCHIC KNOWING)

> Betsy was driving her regular route to work when she just knew there was an accident ahead of her. She slammed on her brakes, even though no obvious reason existed. She slowed down, while the car ahead of her continued at the regular speed. Minutes down the road, the car in front of her was "T-boned" by a car running the stop light.
>
> Gardening was a favorite hobby, and this year Anna put in a bigger vegetable garden. She was working the soil to prepare it for planting, when a strong knowing hit her to check on her father. Her parents were living with her now that they were older, but it was her mother who was ill. She raced inside the house, and her dad was flat on the floor, having tripped on a rug.

When I first started doing readings, I was mostly clairvoyant. I would see something and then go further into it psychically to get more insights for my client. I also used clairsentience and clairaudience, but claircognizance, immediate knowing, wasn't a part of my readings. Like Betsy and Anna, I experienced claircognizance with premonitions, fore-warnings about something that would soon happen. It was always negative and, most of the time, I couldn't change the outcome.

Over the years, my readings became mostly claircognizant. I just know something about my client, and I keep talking until I've shared it all. I use the other "clairs" to expand on what I get with claircognizance. I remember how difficult it was in the beginning to just say what I was getting when it didn't have an image, feeling, or thought associated with it. The other "clairs" seemed more tangible than claircognizance. Based on my experience with students, I think claircognizance may be the apex of psychic ability when the sense is fully developed. This needs to be researched further, as I know that some of my students seem to be naturally claircognizant and have difficulty using the other "clairs."

Definition: (French. *clair*=clear and *conoissance*=knowledge)

Claircognizance refers to the ability to get information just by knowing. It is the ability to know something without input from your rational mind or from observing the world around you. Claircognizance is an immediate knowing without the use of the other "clairs." It just comes—you just know. It is quicker than the other "clairs."

Claircognizance will get stronger when you allow yourself to say whatever comes to you, without analyzing or thinking about it first. When reading something, you just open your mouth and let it flow out as fast as you can. Claircognizance takes a lot of guts, because you have to set aside any fear or anxiety about being wrong, or being judged, or not making sense. You will need a strong self-esteem to use claircognizance. Interestingly, as you take the leap and use it, your self-esteem will grow beyond what you feel is possible—even if you think you already have a strong self-esteem.

Exercise to Increase Claircognizance:

FOCUS ON CLAIRCOGNIZANCE

As you go about your day, think about being claircognizant—that you can immediately know something using your psychic sense. Here are some suggestions:

- Pause at times, and say to yourself, "I am claircognizant; I just know!"

- At other times, tell yourself it's okay to be claircognizant, "I give myself permission to be claircognizant!"

Notice the times you immediately know something. Perhaps spend one day recording in a notebook the times when you immediately knew something—it just came to you. Increase your ability by recognizing it.

What was your experience?

_____
_____
_____
_____
_____
_____
_____
_____
_____
_____
_____
_____
_____
_____
_____
_____
_____
_____
_____
_____
_____
_____
_____
_____
_____
_____
_____
_____

Exercise to Increase Claircognizance:

Doing exercises fast prevents your conscious mind and other "clairs" from assisting you. Fast reading forces you to rely on just knowing.

FAST READING OF A DECK OF CARDS

Relax jaw, take a breath, connect with your body; are you relaxed?

Get a deck of regular playing cards. Place the 10 of Hearts and a 10 of Clubs face up. Then pick a card from the deck, quickly read the color, and place it face down on the black or red pile depending upon what color you know it to be. Continue until the entire deck is read. Do this without thinking, and do it fast!

When you are finished, see how you did. Even better, work your claircognizant "muscle" over and over for two weeks WITHOUT looking at how you did. This will strengthen your claircognizance because you will be focused on doing claircognizance rather than on a need to see if you are right.

What was your experience?

The Akashic Records

Definition: Akasha: *Sanskrit,* sky, space, aether.
Akashic Records: boundless space; the Book of Life; Hall of Records; soul record.

One of the best ways to increase claircognizance is to read the Akashic Records. It doesn't matter whether you believe such a record exists. The method provides a great way to enhance claircognizance, because information typically comes much faster than when using other methods.

The origins of the records can be found in many cultures under varying names. Ancient Hebrews, Greeks, and Egyptians believed a record of all history existed and, for some, it included a list of those eligible for entrance into heaven. In the nineteenth century, Theosophy held the idea that an energetic record existed of all knowledge and experience—everything. Early twentieth-century psychic Edgar Cayce astral traveled to the Hall of Records to read a person's soul record.

Some may see the Akashic Records as an account of the fate of the universe—viewing human experience as set in stone. But another way of viewing this is that many future possibilities exist, and all are recorded in the Akashic Records. By reading the Akashic Record, you can sense what possibilities are most likely being played out, giving the options and likely outcomes. This view is empowering, unlike the concept that everything in our lives has already been planned or fated.

The Akashic Records provide another way to approach reading a person or situation. Since they provide an energetic record of everything, you can use it to read anything. Often these records are accessed to obtain assistance with life direction and deeper insights into one's soul.

HOW TO ACCESS THE AKASHIC RECORDS:

1. Relax, ground, and center yourself.

2. When you are in that centered state, use your breath to further relax your body. You might try breathing without a pause between breaths. Do this without taking in deep breaths or controlling your breath in any way. At some point, your body will likely feel lighter. If you feel dizzy, put your breath and thoughts in your feet, and put your hand on your solar plexus. When you feel more grounded, begin again.

3. Put your focus on the top of your head. Breathe with the top of your head until you sense it open. Then move your awareness and breathe up and out of your head going quickly up an energetic tube or tunnel that continues beyond you. This tube of energy will take you to the Akashic Records. Maintain your focus and intention of going up the tube to the Akashic Records.

4. Enter the Akashic Records. You will likely experience the Akashic Records differently from others, and you might find your own perception changes over time. A being or spirit will probably greet you. I prefer to call this the Reference Librarian. At times, you might ask to be shown around and be given a tour and information on how to access the records.

The "record" might be a book, file, scroll, MP3 download, or any kind of format. It's all energy, so whatever form it comes in isn't as important as connecting with the energy.

5. Ask for a record. I usually ask the Reference Librarian to give me the record on a person, event, or issue. If necessary, I ask for assistance to understand the record.

6. Bring the record back down the tube of energy and into your head. I have a knowing deep inside me that when the Akashic record enters into my head, I know what is important to know about my client. Here are some tips:

"Hold" the Akashic record in your "hands" and get a feel for its weight, thickness, emotion, and whatever else comes to you.

Then open the record to the place that tells you what you need to know at this time. If you need help with this, ask the Reference Librarian.

Allow impressions to come to you about what is in the record.

Speak—let the record speak through you. Don't filter and think about what you are saying. Just let it flow smoothly and simply.

7. When you are finished reading the record, return it to the Akashic Records. Visualize the record going quickly out of the top of your head, up the energetic tube, and to the great library in the sky.

8. Close the top of your head. Return to your body, and pull your awareness back into the room you are in. Reading the Akashic Records is different than reading the energy around a person. I am typically less connected to the client and to my physical environment when I access the Akashic Records. But I keep enough connection during the reading so that I am balanced—since this is not a channeling session.

REFERENCES:

Crystal Links. www.crystalinks.com/akashicrecords.html
Edgar Cayce. www.edgarcayce.org/are/spiritualGrowth.aspx?id=2078
Linda Howe. www.akashicstudies.com/. *How to Read the Akashic Records: Accessing the Archive of the Soul and Its Journey.* by Linda Howe, 2009

Create Your Package!

TIP FOR GOOD ETHICS:	Sometimes psychic insights will just come to you about your family or friends—without your seeking them. When this happens, you have to decide what's best: to tell or not to tell. If you think it's important, you could share the information without saying that you got it psychically. Be careful about undercutting a person's own good judgment.

Exercise to Increase Claircognizance:

ACCESS YOUR AKASHIC RECORD

Relax jaw, take a breath, connect with your body; are you relaxed?

Use the instructions to get a record from the Akashic Records that pertains to you. When you have the record in your hands, speak out loud what it feels like (weight, thickness, emotion, and whatever else comes to you). Then "open" the record to the information you could best use now. Speak out loud what you get. Complete the remaining steps from the instructions.

What was your experience?

_____

_____

_____

_____

_____

_____

_____

_____

_____

_____

Answers to Your Question

READ USING CLAIRCOGNIZANCE:
AUTOMATIC WRITING

Get in that connected, quiet zone. Connect to a spirit guide or to your higher/expanded self. Hold the expectation that this guide or your expanded self is going to give you insights about the question you've been using for this workbook.

Then just start writing for ten minutes without thinking about it or stopping. Don't concern yourself with grammar, spelling, punctuation—that just keeps you in your conscious, thinking mind. Hold the expectation as you write that you will not stop at all, so that you force yourself to get past any glitches in writing. If you find yourself unable to think of something to write, this means you are thinking and not being psychic! If you feel stuck, just try writing the same word over and over until something else comes.

Write this on your paper or type it onto a computer screen:

(Spirit guide or Expanded self) tell me a story that will help me with my question about:

_____

_____

_____

_____

_____

_____

_____

_____

_____

_____

_____

_____

_____

_____

Record insights in your journal. Reflect on this writing over the next day or two, making notes about how it is speaking to you. Every time you pay attention to your psychic insights, you improve your psychic skills. Sometimes "hard" thinking isn't required—just hold this exercise lightly in your mind and contemplate on what you got.

Dreamwork

Remember to paint your dreams

Get watercolors, crayons, colored pencils, paper, or other art material.

Paint or color something about a dream, like an abstract picture of how your dream makes you feel or a more detailed drawing of a specific part of your dream.

Put the date of the dream on the back.

Paint something about your dreams on a regular basis. Later in the workbook, you will be given instructions on what to do with your pictures. For now, just paint or color your dreams. You will need at least ten pictures.

5 Clairalience

(PSYCHIC SMELLING)

> Mattie came for a reading, and after giving her insights about her job, I sensed a spirit around her. "Your mother has passed." Mattie nodded yes. She seemed too young to have lost her mom. I gave Mattie a message from her mother and moved on to questions she had brought for the reading. As I continued, an overwhelming smell of alcohol filled the room. I have allergies, so sometimes it takes me a while to smell things. So, I just figured I was late in smelling that my client had been drinking. I wondered if my client had an alcohol problem. At that point in my reading career, I was uncomfortable bringing up such personal issues. But the smell would not go away.
>
> The scent, however, got even stronger, so I had to pay attention. When I paused to ask silently what this was about, a wave of an alcohol smell came flowing from Mattie's mother in spirit. I stopped what I had been focusing on and said, "Your mom was a drinker."
>
> Mattie confirmed this. We were able to explore her relationship and current life struggles more fully because I had acknowledged the psychic smell of alcohol. Her mother apologized to her daughter for harm she had caused. Tears filled Mattie's eyes, and she was grateful to hear these words from her mother, as she had not been capable of hearing this apology when she was alive.

Definition: (French. *clair*=clear and *alience*=smelling)

Clairalience refers to the ability to get information by smelling psychically. This includes being able to smell something without the odor actually being present.

Clairalience and clairgustance are typically used less often, but they can be developed like any aspect of the psychic sense. Improving these secondary "clairs" will strengthen your primary "clairs." Try using either psychic smelling or tasting when you are stuck using the other "clairs." This may help you get past the block and, in the process, strengthen your psychic sense.

In my experience, clairalience is often associated with spirit communication. Students and clients regularly tell me about smelling the favorite perfume or cologne of loved ones who have passed. For a friend of mine, clairalience became a signal when someone close to her was about to die.

Ella's favorite cat Bootsie died. Bootsie had been listless and refusing to eat for a week. The vet found her intestines riddled with cancer and telephoned my friend to see how she wanted to proceed. Ella knew she had to let Bootsie go, and then shortly after the telephone call ended, she was overwhelmed by the odor of kitty litter. For the next several days after Bootsie died, she would suddenly experience suffused all around her the odor of kitty litter. Bootsie had rarely used a litter box, preferring to go outside, and the house had never smelled like cat litter. I suggested to Ella that this was Bootsie's way of letting her know she was on the "other side" and doing fine.

The communication from Bootsie didn't end there. We sometimes have a very special connection to particular animals, and Bootsie was one of those for Ella. A few months later, the cat next door kept coming into Ella's garage to lie on the floor. One night, about seven in the evening, the overwhelming smell of kitty litter filled the house. Ella exclaimed that it meant the neighbor's cat had just died. The next day, the neighbor came over and told Ella her cat had died just about the same time my friend had smelled the litter.

This experience seemed to open Ella's psychic abilities further. Bootsie's presence around her in spirit may be what facilitated this, as several psychics have seen Bootsie with Ella, including myself. Ella now gets odors clairaliently when someone she is close to dies.

One evening, Ella suddenly smelled cigarette smoke all around her. It was as though someone was exhaling and blowing the smoke in her direction. The odor was so strong that Ella looked out her bedroom window thinking someone was in the park behind her house smoking a cigarette. But she saw no one. The odor around her was overwhelming, just as it had been with the kitty litter when Bootsie died. The next morning, as she was cooking breakfast, she smelled it again. By this time, Ella was pretty sure she was being given a message—but she had no idea what it meant.

Then she received an email that a beloved friend had passed, and she had been a smoker. It seems spirits find any way to communicate with us. This is particularly interesting since Ella's friend held the belief that after you depart, there is nothing. I've spoken with more than one spirit over the years who also held this belief. And yet they are there communicating with me.

Exercise to Increase Clairalience:

FOCUS ON WHAT YOU SMELL

As you go about your day, focus on what you smell. This will carry over to your psychic sense. Here are some suggestions:

- Pause at times, and focus on your nose. Pay special attention to the quality of aroma in the room.
- Sense smelling more fully. Sense the subtle smells that are around you all the time—your odor, others' body odor, the outdoors.

What was your experience?

_____

_____

_____

_____

_____

_____

_____

_____

_____

_____

_____

_____

WHAT SMELL IS IN THE CONTAINER?

Wrap separately three items that have an obvious smell in plastic wrap and/or paper so you can't see what the item is. Place each item in a container. You can get a friend or family member to do this for you if you'd like.

Get in that connected, quiet zone. Put your awareness inside your nose. Wiggle your nose. Breathe with your nose consciousness—not the same as breathing—it's being aware of your nose/smell psychically. Let a smell enter your nose. What do you psychically smell in each of the containers?

What was your experience?

_____

_____

_____

_____

_____

_____

_____

Exercise to Increase Clairalience:
INCLUDE PSYCHIC SMELLING IN EVERYDAY LIVING

Use clairalience to get information to understand experiences you are having. Examples: You are at work listening to a co-worker talk about a project or talking about personal matters. You are at a store looking for an item or standing in line at the checkout. You are on the phone with a family member or friend.

Pause, and remember that you can get helpful information through your clairalience. Ask, silently to yourself, for a smell to give you additional insights about what is being discussed. Let it come to you. If you get something, go back into the smell and ask what it means. Don't interpret it with your conscious, analytical mind.

Disconnect by pulling your energy away from the person or situation.

Do this for one day.

What was your experience?

_____

_____

_____

_____

_____

_____

_____

_____

_____

_____

_____

_____

_____

_____

_____

_____

_____

_____

_____

_____

_____

_____

_____

_____

_____

_____

_____

_____

_____

_____

_____

READ USING CLAIRALIENCE

Get in that connected, quiet zone. Put your awareness inside your nose. Wiggle your nose. Breathe with your nose consciousness—not the same as breathing—it's being aware of your nose/smell psychically. Think about your question. Let a smell enter your nose. Make a note of the smell.

Put your awareness back into the smell that came to you. Be present there for a few moments. When you feel connected to it, ask what the smell means, "What does this smell have to do with my question about…?"

Stay out of your conscious, analytical mind. For example, if you got a putrid smell, don't assume it means the answer to your question is negative. Ask the smell for more insights. You just might be surprised at what you get.

Record insights in your journal. No matter what insights you received from psychic smelling, make a tentative guess at what the smell is communicating about your question. What one step could you take based on what you got? Even the smallest step gives you stronger psychic skills.

6 Clairgustance

(PSYCHIC TASTING)

> I don't use clairgustance in my psychic reading practice. On occasion, I've used the other secondary "clair," clairalience/smelling. But never psychic tasting. I was preparing for a class while writing this workbook, and I figured I should practice what I teach and put more emphasis on the two lesser "clairs." Thinking I would do this when life slowed down, I put it out of my mind.
>
> A few days later, Margaret came for a reading. She was a new client, and I felt immediately drawn to her health, though we had been talking about the repairs being done to her house. A strong sense of coffee filled the back of my mouth. Odd, because I don't drink coffee— never developed a taste for it. I'm a tea drinker. But that day, I tasted coffee.
>
> Then I tasted coffee in my gut—really tasted it there. I don't know how to explain this, because I know logically that intestines cannot taste. But that's what happened.
>
> Quickly after tasting strong coffee, my claircognizance kicked in, and I blurted out to my client, "You drink a lot of coffee!" She admitted that she did and that she was planning to cut down the amount. I went back into the clairgustance I was sensing and gave her more insights about her health and what was going on in her life. The insights I shared were not my opinion. I gave her psychic insights—insights that originated from psychically tasting the overabundance of coffee she had been drinking.

I put no effort into having that clairgustance experience. Yes, I am a professional psychic, and I have been doing readings for years. But I'm not special. Anyone can learn this and improve their natural psychic abilities. So, just think lightly about this, or another "clair," and see what happens!

Definition: (French. *clair*=clear and *gustance*=tasting)

Clairgustance refers to the ability to get information by tasting psychically. This includes being able to taste something without putting it in the mouth. As with all the "clairs," put your energy awareness with what you psychically taste, and ask it for more insights.

I really do want you to set aside your conscious, thinking, advice-giving mind and connect psychically to get information. Every time you set aside your thinking, analytical mind and go back into the energy of what you got psychically and then ask for more psychic insights, your psychic "muscle" gets stronger. Doing this may be slow in the beginning. But what you get in the end is a strong psychic sense.

Exercise to Increase Clairgustance:

FOCUS ON WHAT YOU TASTE

As you go about your day, focus on your mouth, both when eating and not. This will carry over to your psychic sense. Here are some suggestions:

- Pause at times, and focus on your mouth. Get a sense of taste about feelings, people, and experiences. Just play/pretend with this, and notice how much more you taste.

- Sense tasting more fully. Sense the subtle tastes of your food and that are around you all the time.

What was your experience?

_____
_____
_____
_____
_____
_____
_____
_____
_____
_____
_____
_____
_____
_____
_____
_____
_____
_____
_____
_____
_____
_____
_____
_____
_____
_____
_____
_____
_____
_____
_____
_____
_____
_____
_____
_____

Exercise to Increase Clairgustance:

WHAT TASTE IS IN THE CONTAINER?

Get three food items that have an obvious taste. Wrap each of the items in plastic wrap and/or paper, so you can't smell or see what the item is. Place each item in a container. You can get a friend or family member to do this for you, if you'd like.

Use clairgustance to psychically sense what food item is inside a plastic container. Get in that connected, quiet zone. Put your awareness inside your mouth. Wiggle your tongue. Be with your mouth/tongue consciousness. Let a taste enter your mouth. What do you psychically taste in each of the three containers?

What was your experience?

_____
_____
_____
_____
_____
_____
_____
_____
_____
_____
_____
_____
_____
_____
_____
_____
_____
_____
_____
_____
_____
_____
_____
_____
_____
_____
_____
_____
_____
_____
_____

Exercise to Increase Clairgustance:

INCLUDE PSYCHIC TASTING IN EVERYDAY LIVING

Use clairgustance to get additional information to understand experiences you are having. Examples: You are at work listening to a co-worker talk about a project or talking about personal matters. You are at a store looking for an item or standing in line at the checkout. You are on the phone with a family member or friend.

Pause and remember that you can get helpful information through your clairgustance. Ask, silently to yourself, for a taste to give you additional insights about what is being discussed. Let it come to you. If you get something, go back into the taste and ask what it means. Don't interpret it with your conscious, analytical mind.

Disconnect by jumping up and down.

Do this for one day.

What was your experience?

_____

_____

_____

_____

_____

_____

_____

_____

_____

_____

_____

Answers to Your Question

READ USING CLAIRGUSTANCE

Get in that connected, quiet zone. Put your awareness inside your mouth. Wiggle your tongue. Be with your mouth/tongue consciousness. Think about your question. Let a taste enter your mouth. Make a note of the taste.

Put your awareness back into the taste that came to you. Be present there for a few moments. When you feel connected to it, ask what the taste means, "What does this taste have to do with my question about…?"

Stay out of your conscious, analytical mind. For example, if you get a sweet taste, don't assume it means the answer to your question is positive. Ask the taste for more insights. You may be surprised.

Record insights in your journal. It's okay if you didn't get a lot from this exercise. Just write about what you did get, and then take a minor step in response to what you think your psychic tasting is telling you. Be playful with your psychic sense. Take tentative steps based on the psychic information you receive. This primes the pump for you to get more psychic insights the next time you use your psychic skills.

Create Your Package!

TIP FOR GROUNDING: Put your energy and attention with yourself for a few moments. Just feel your awareness, being with yourself.

7 "Running Your Clairs"

Now that you have exercised your psychic "clairs," try using all of them when you want to get insights. When teaching in the Aspen Program, Marcia Stanfield called this "Running Your Clairs." It's a wonderful way to think about how to use your "clairs" fully and effectively—run through them all when you have a question to get the most from your psychic ability!

Your Question:

_____
_____
_____
_____
_____
_____
_____
_____
_____
_____
_____

CLAIRSENTIENCE – PSYCHIC FEELING (EMOTIONS & ENERGY)
What do I feel about this?

CLAIRVOYANCE – PSYCHIC SEEING
What do I see about this?

CLAIRAUDIENCE – PSYCHIC HEARING
What do I hear about this?

CLAIRCOGNIZANCE – PSYCHIC KNOWING
What do I know about this?

CLAIRGUSTANCE – PSYCHIC TASTING
Is there a taste associated with this?

CLAIRALIENCE – PSYCHIC SMELLING
Is there a scent or odor associated with this?

Breathe ...

The Seven Major Chakras

ALSO KNOWN AS THE MAJOR ENERGY CENTERS IN THE BODY

CROWN CHAKRA
Pituitary gland—Violet

THIRD EYE CHAKRA
Pineal gland—Indigo

THROAT CHAKRA
Thyroid gland—Blue

HEART CHAKRA
Thymus gland—Green

SOLAR PLEXUS CHAKRA
Adrenal glands—Yellow

SPLENIC CHAKRA
Spleen—Orange

ROOT CHAKRA
Gonads (ovaries & testes)—Red

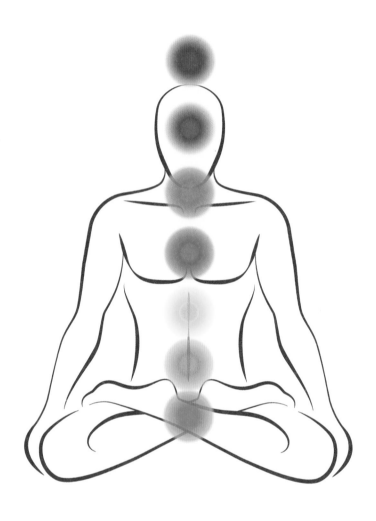

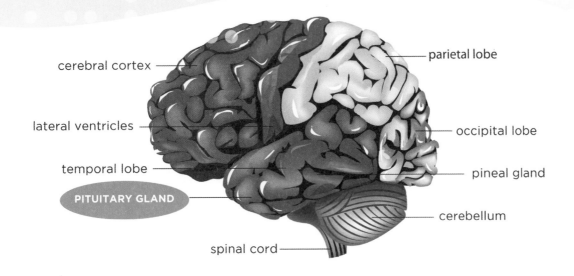

cerebral cortex

parietal lobe

lateral ventricles

occipital lobe

temporal lobe

pineal gland

PITUITARY GLAND

cerebellum

spinal cord

Crown Chakra Breathing

Do this throughout your day except when driving or other times when you need to pay attention.

Get comfortable and relax. Take a deep breath, and let it out with a sigh. Open your jaw a bit at the hinge, feel your shoulders relax, sense your body releasing into your chair or where you are standing.

Put your attention on the top of your head. Pretend a door or hatch is on the top of your head. Open this with your intention. Breathe in and out of the top of your head. Visualize and actually feel the breath going in and out of the top of the head.

Breathe with your pituitary gland. After you have clearly sensed the Crown Chakra breathing, move your awareness down into your brain and breathe with the pituitary gland. It is in the center of your brain and is the size of a pea, shaped like a kidney bean. Your awareness will find it, and you will get a sense of its physical and energetic characteristics. Continue breathing, feeling the Crown Chakra opening.

Say to yourself (or out loud), "I am psychic." This affirmative statement works with the unconscious mind to open your innate psychic sense. Say this while breathing with your Crown Chakra.

Ground yourself after this exercise by closing the top of your head, like a hatch closing. Breathe with your feet and the Earth.

NOTES

NOTES

CHAPTER 4

It's Easier Than You Think

7 Approaches to Psychic Development

Approaches to Psychic Development

1. Mental Focus (Quiet your mind)
2. Body Awareness (Sense your body's wisdom)
3. Play Outside Your Rut (Shift your brain)
4. Dreams (Guidance as you sleep)
5. Creativity (Use your imagination—it's psychic!)
6. Nature Awareness (Be present with Nature)
7. Games (Have fun!)

When I created the Aspen Program for Psychic Development, I made a list of what I had been doing since I was a child that I thought had contributed to my being psychic. These seven approaches are the result. Consider what helps open your psychic sense and incorporate this in your learning process as well.

Please don't think you have to do everything in this section. Pick and choose what works for you, morphing it to fit what's best for you. Psychic development is a personal journey. Take the information, integrate some of it into your daily life, and make it yours by changing it to fit your needs and way of doing things. Your inner guidance will help you with this. As your psychic sense gets stronger, allow it to teach you new ways of developing your abilities. The following are just tools, and they will probably need to be revised or replaced with newer ways of working with your psychic sense as you move further along in your development.

Many paths will take you to your psychic sense, and it's best to work with them all. Be consistent and persistent when working with the following seven approaches. If you don't see improvements in your ability to connect with your psychic sense within three to six months, you will likely need to take steps to discover what may be blocking your abilities.

Also included in this section are additional techniques to get psychic answers to the question you chose at the beginning of the workbook. At the end of this chapter, you will gather all the psychic insights you have received on this question, and use a psychic technique to decide what the next best steps are for you to take.

Dreamwork

Remember to paint your dreams

Get watercolors, crayons, colored pencils, paper, or other art material.

Paint or color something about a dream, like an abstract picture of how your dream makes you feel or a more detailed drawing of a specific part of your dream.

Put the date of the dream on the back.

Paint something about your dreams on a regular basis. Later in the workbook, you will be given instructions on what to do with your pictures. For now, just paint or color your dreams. You will need at least ten pictures.

1 Mental Focus

QUIET YOUR MIND

At 16, my boyfriend Paul gave me the book, *Be Here Now*, by Ram Dass. It was the early 1970s, and I really liked Paul. So I read books on Eastern religions, the *Bhagavad Gita*, the Upanishads, Patanjali, Krishnamurti—the list is endless. We talked philosophy all the time, the meaning of life, why we are here. I biked to the grove of trees at the Virginia Theological Seminary and read these books by myself or with Paul. Books opened my world to explore new ideas and to discover new passions. I did yoga, meditated, kept a journal, and got into nutrition and holistic healing.

Paul taught me to meditate, and the first type of meditation I did was staring at a candle flame. I thought I was cool. I was fortunate that I grew up in an open-minded Christian home, so it was acceptable for my sisters and me to follow in the Beatles' footsteps and journey down this metaphysical road. That's also when I found Edgar Cayce and read numerous books about his work, particularly his health readings.

Twenty years later, I moved on, having learned to always question "shoulding" rules. My Southern Baptist upbringing, believe it or not, had far less controlling dogma than did some of the groups and material I had been exploring in metaphysics and Eastern religions. In my early twenties, the adults at my Southern Baptist Church asked me to teach them about Buddhism and Hinduism so they could better understand their kids.

I had my son early in life, and that kind of messed up my meditation career. He was hyperactive, so there was little silence in my home. I learned other ways of quieting my mind. Some of them are listed below. I particularly like Rocking Chair Meditation or maybe I should call it Southern Meditation, because we so like our rocking chairs in the South!

The single-most important thing you need to effectively access your psychic abilities is to be able to quiet your mind and body—at will. Your psychic awareness may not be as noticeable at first. As children, we were taught to develop our analytical, rational minds. So, you have to quiet this aspect of your mind to be more psychic. And we all have mind chatter at times, but to be fully psychic, you have to be in control of your mind. When I ask students if they have mind chatter, almost every hand rises. Perhaps in our world today, with all its technological noise devices, mind chatter is the norm. The more important question is: Are you able to turn off the chatter when you want? If you experience a lot of this, be persistent using the techniques below. Your mind will eventually relax, so you can connect with your psychic guidance.

You need to reach the point where you can tune into that quiet, connected zone that is experienced during meditation or physical activity (the runner's high). The goal is to be able to get into that zone quickly, even when there is noise around you, such as ticking clocks. When you can achieve this kind of mental focus, your psychic ability will be there when you need it.

HOW TO DEVELOP A HEALTHY HABIT

Learn how to develop healthy habits, so you can do what you want (like meditation) without having to think about it or force yourself. No one makes you brush your teeth; it has become a regular part of your day. It is important to get to the point where quieting your mind and using your psychic sense is a natural, effortless part of your day. The following method can be used for developing any good habit.

Decide what habit you want to establish. For example, using a mental focus technique daily.

Make a list of the types you enjoy. You are more likely to use the techniques you like to do. Choose from those in this workbook, as well as from your own experiences.

Decide how often and what time of day to develop the habit.

Give yourself permission to practice the habit for only one minute, if that's all you want to do. The point isn't how long you do it. The point is for you to do it each time you have chosen to do so. Don't punish yourself for practicing your chosen habit for only a short period of time.

For example, you may decide to meditate every morning and mid-afternoon. You are doing fairly well at this, but, one morning, you just don't have the time to settle yourself to meditate. So, sit where you normally do to meditate. Close your eyes, take a deep breath and let it out, relaxing your mind and body. Pause, and if you decide that's all the time you have, or you just don't want to do any more, then get up and get going with your day. The point is to do the habit—not focus on the length of time. You also can choose a different item from your list of mental focusing techniques. This prevents boredom and gives you choice.

Tools to Increase Your Mental Focus

Spend quiet alone time each day. Spend time by yourself without reading or noise of any kind (sometimes soothing music is okay). Your mind may wander and think about the day or issues in your life. That's fine; allow this to happen. But wait until your mind is clear, sitting alone, without noise, without thinking. There will come a space in this quiet alone-time when you will hear your inner voice.

Create a psychic room. Create in your mind a place where you go to connect with your inner resources and do psychic work. Your psychic room can be anything you would like, such as a garden or a room with all the necessary equipment you need, like a movie screen, a remote control, and a special helper guide. You can always modify the room later, and you may find that at some point you no longer require this.

Meditation. A variety of books, classes, MP3s, and techniques for meditation are available today. Try them until you find ones that suit you. Here are some suggestions:

1. **Do head rolls before meditation.** Gently roll your head three times in a clockwise circle, being careful not to overextend your head. Then roll your head counterclockwise three times. Open your jaw at the hinge, relax your shoulders, remember to breathe, and begin meditation. Some think head rolls stimulate the pineal and pituitary glands that connect with your psychic sense.

2. **Candle Meditation.** If you are having difficulty emptying your mind of thoughts, try staring at a candle flame. This gives you something to do, so you will likely find it easier to focus. If your mind wanders, just return your focus to observing the flame.

3. **Metronome Meditation.** Stare at the movement of the metronome's pendulum or just listen to the ticking. Metronomes are available online for viewing, but staring at a computer screen might tire your eyes—you could just listen to the clicking sound to stay focused. You can find metronomes where musical instruments are sold.

4. **Mantra Meditation.** While in meditation, use a mantra (one word or a short phrase) to repeat silently to yourself, *e.g.*, "peace." When your mind wanders, just repeat the mantra a few times, or you can repeat the mantra every few seconds throughout meditation.

5. **Practice Presence—Mindfulness Meditation.** As you go through your day, be in the moment of what you are doing. If you are cutting vegetables for a salad, turn off the television or other noise, and focus on cutting each vegetable. If you garden, focus your mind and energy on gardening. If you are walking, focus on feeling your body moving. Knitting, needlepoint, or similar crafts are also ways to quiet your mind, as long as you are only focused on what you are doing. Being in the moment is a way of entering a meditative state at almost any time. Let go of thoughts about other things, and focus your attention on what you are doing or experiencing.

6. **Rocking Chair Meditation.** This technique comes from my Southern roots—rocking in a rocking chair on the porch on a nice day. The back and forth movement facilitates relaxation. You can spend time thinking about your day, your concerns, and your plans as you rock. At some point, you will be finished

processing your thoughts. Your mind will be emptied enough for you to access your expanded awareness. Leave your eyes open (if you close them, you'll likely get sleepy). Continue to rock (or not) and be in a space of emptiness. You cannot force a meditative state; you have to allow it to come to you. So, if you have thoughts and really want to process them, go ahead and do that while you rock. After using this technique frequently, you will find that you have fewer things to think about and can more quickly enter into a quiet space of just being. This kind of meditation can allow for inspirational or contemplative thought once your mind is still.

7. **Breath Meditation.** Observe your breath without controlling it. As you observe your breath, it will take you deeper into meditation.

8. **Spinal Breathing Pranayama.** This is a technique for breathing along the nerve that runs from your perineum up your spine and over the top of your head to your third-eye. The perineum is the space between the genitals and the anus. See *Spinal Breathing Pranayama: Journey to Inner Space*, by Yogani. This book is a must read if you want to use this technique, with my modifications: As you breathe in slowly, imagine your breath is moving an elevator from your perineum, up the sacrum, up your spine (every inch), neck, back of your head, over the top of your head to your third-eye. Breathe out, bringing the elevator back down to your perineum. The book explains the *hows* and *whys* and methods to protect yourself—so get the book.

Hypnosis. Knowing how to enter into a light trance is helpful in psychic work. If you are having difficulty quieting your mind, try hypnosis. A variety of recordings are available for hypnosis, meditation, and relaxation. Be sure to listen to the recording first to see if it fits with your beliefs and the voice is soothing to you. A good resource for recordings is www.healthjourneys.com. Bookstores usually have a wide range of meditation and relaxation CDs.

1. **Use recordings before going to sleep.** One of the best times for sending messages to your unconscious mind is the time just before entering sleep, called the hypnagogic state.

2. **Recordings should be a supplement, not a replacement, for meditation.** If you are having difficulty meditating, start with recordings and then later try meditating without them. At some point, you should be able to meditate without the use of an aid.

Journaling. Keeping a journal provides you with a place to go to process your life experiences. By writing in your journal on a regular basis, you are better able to empty your mind of self-talk and worry. Journaling is a way to quiet your mind.

A good habit to establish is to begin your day by writing every thought that comes into your mind immediately upon waking. This can capture insights from your dreams, and it clears your mind so you can focus on your day.

Exercise to Increase Clairvoyance:

COLOR FLASH CARDS.
(Individual or pairs)

Relax jaw, take a breath, connect with your body; are you relaxed?

Get a regular deck of playing cards. Visualize a movie screen in front of your face. Read the color of each card, expecting red or black to flash on the screen. If you play this in pairs, the person holding the card sends the color to the reader's screen. Read the entire deck and then check to see how you did. Try this exercise with your eyes open and then closed to see what works best for you.

_____
_____
_____
_____
_____
_____
_____
_____
_____
_____
_____

Create Your Package!

TIP FOR BOUNDARIES:

Put your energy inside one of your chakras. How does it feel?

Smile. Be present there for a few moments.

How does that chakra feel now?

Answers to Your Question

READ USING CLAIRVOYANCE

Pair up and get into that connected, quiet zone. Do a short reading of each other's question that you are using for this workbook:

1. Focus your gaze to the left of your partner, between her/his head and right shoulder. See a movie screen there.

2. Breathe with the occipital lobe of your brain at the back of your head.

3. When your eyes glaze over, allow images to come to you about the question.

4. **Share the images you get with your partner—without interpretation.**

   - When you get a psychic image, focus on the image and ask the image questions to get more information.

   - **DO NOT analyze or interpret what you get with your conscious mind.** Do not try to understand what you are getting. Just share everything you get.

   - Go back into the image and ask it to give you more psychic information.

5. When you are finished receiving psychic insights, discuss the possible meanings and significance of the images with your partner.

For individuals: Stare at a blank wall—white is best. Move your eyes to your left, and imagine a movie screen on the wall. If visualizing doesn't come easy for you, try actually looking at a television or computer screen that isn't on. Breathe with the occipital lobe of your brain. When your eyes glaze over, allow images to come to you about your question. Continue with the instructions in #4 and #5 above.

Record insights in your journal. When you have made notes about your clairvoyant insights, select what you think is the best answer to your question. Carry the image of that answer around with you over the next day or two. Return to your journal to record further insights. Later in the workbook, you will bring together all the insights for the sections, "Answers to Your Question." Perhaps this exercise will be clearer to you at that time.

2 Body Awareness

SENSE YOUR BODY'S WISDOM

One year to the day that my grandmother died, she visited me in my dreams. I was sitting in a rocking chair and, just like in "Whistler's Mother," there was a painting on the wall to the right of me.

I looked up at it, and the ghostly face of my grandmother appeared over the painting's image. I was freaked by this, particularly as she started talking with me. She said that I had exhibited psychic ability as a child and that my mother would know about this. Then she went on to give me a list of my psychic abilities. When I woke, I only recalled one item from the list, and that led me to go to massage school where I got my body awareness back. I had left it behind in childhood.

I attended Potomac Massage Training Institute in Washington, D.C., although I had taken two massage classes six years earlier just as the Cayce/Reilly School of Massotherapy was forming in Virginia Beach. Massage school was one-and-a-half years, part-time, which gave students plenty of time to figure out what was going on in our own bodies. They always said, "You can only take your client where you have been yourself." I am fortunate to have attended PMTI. It was a positive turning point in both my life and psychic abilities.

During the first six-month semester, I started seeing images when I massaged homework clients. My first experience was while massaging Diane. I looked up from massaging her arm to see a nun standing on the other side of the table, dressed in full-habit clothing. Her head was bowed, so I couldn't see her face. Her slender hands were pearlescent, folded gently across her abdomen, and slid partially inside the sleeves of her habit.

I was taken aback. I figured I wasn't really seeing this, because I didn't see it with my "naked" eyes. I put it out of my mind and continued with the massage. But the image kept coming back, no matter where I was working on Diane's body. The nun never said or did anything. Back then, I didn't know what to do about such an image. Today, I would know to put my energy awareness with it and ask what it was about.

I hadn't known Diane for long, so I was apprehensive about telling her about this. Finally, because the nun wouldn't go away, I figured it must be important. After the massage was completed, I hesitantly told her that I kept seeing an image during the session. Diane encouraged me to tell her more, so I told her that I had seen a nun. Diane burst into tears. I was astonished. What could possibly be going on, I wondered. I knew enough from other training to give Diane time to process this. Then she told me that she felt like a cloistered nun throughout her marriage. We talked about this, and I was glad that I had told her what I had seen.

We were required to submit a log describing our homework sessions. I included my psychic experiences, like the one with Diane, but I never received any feedback. I finally asked my teacher why, and she said the teachers didn't know what do to with my experiences. I eventually figured it out with some help from a psychic. By halfway through the program, I'd guess that about half the students were having psychic experiences. I have met other professional psychics who also found their abilities opened in massage school.

Your body is a vehicle for connecting with your psychic sense. Body awareness is psychic awareness, and the more you connect with the energy, emotions, and insights in your body, the easier it is to be psychic. You have already learned how to put your energy awareness into your occipital and temporal lobes. This same technique can be used to put your energy awareness into whatever you want to read, whether it is another person, the future, and even a question you have.

We all had more body awareness as children. Our bodies reacted to people, situations, and food. Just watch a young child, and you'll see how their bodies make sense of their surroundings. Most of us were taught to straighten our bodies and make them be quiet, civilized. The consequence was that our body knowing became quashed through more rational, tangible knowing and cultural norms.

Tools to Increase Your Body Awareness

Physical Exercise. Our bodies need regular exercise, not only for good physical health but for mental health. For example, you might use walking to "walk out" your problems, thinking about them as you use this form of exercise. At some point, your mind will empty, and walking will become a meditative experience. Some types of exercise are particularly helpful in being more body aware. Do exercises that are slower and require mindfulness as you do them. Select exercises where you are aware of the movement of energy in and around your body, such as Qi Gong, Tai Chi, and Yoga.

The Seven Major Chakras

ALSO KNOWN AS THE MAJOR ENERGY CENTERS IN THE BODY

Chakra Clearing Exercise

THIS TECHNIQUE BRINGS CLEARING AND BALANCE TO THE CHAKRAS.

1. **Look at a picture of the seven major chakras** in the body, so that you can locate their positions. Or just go with your intuitive connection to them.
2. **Relax.** Close your eyes, take in a deep breath, and let it out; open your jaw at the hinge, feeling the muscles relax from your jaw down your body.
3. **Starting with the root chakra, move your awareness to the circle of energy in your pelvic region.** You might want to place your hand on your chakra.
4. **Breathe with the chakra.**
5. **What do you sense?** Look for color, movement, vibration, sound, words, and images. You might not experience the typical colors of the chakras—different philosophies exist about the chakra system and the colors vary.
6. **Smile; physically smile.** How does your chakra feel now?
7. **Continue with this exercise, moving up through all seven chakras in the body.**
8. **Now breathe with all the seven chakras at once,** feeling the unity of energy within and around your body. Then turn up the corners of your mouth in a soft smile. Notice the shift in the energy.
9. **Get in the habit of connecting to your chakras throughout your day.** Tune into a chakra, and ask how it is doing.

Breathe ...

Whole Body Breathing

This is one of the best ways to get in touch with your body.

1. **Get comfortable.** This exercise can be done in any position, but it might be helpful to start with lying down. Close your eyes, take in a deep breath, and let it out with a sigh. Open your jaw at the hinge, feeling the muscles relax from your jaw down the length of your body.

    To relax the body even more, tighten and relax each body part one at a time:

    Squeeze both feet.

    Tighten both legs.

    Pull in the buttocks.

    Pull in the stomach while squeezing the upper chest and shoulders.

    Tighten both arms and hands.

    Squish the face, including the ears.

    Now, tighten the whole body and relax.

2. **Watch your breath.** There is no need to control or increase your breath. Just watch your breath as it goes in and out of your body. It will soften and slow down on its own.

3. **Breathe with your whole body.** Shift your awareness now to your whole body. Visualize your body as a lung, expanding and contracting, as if your skin moves slightly in and out as you breathe. Or try visualizing every pore of your body taking in breath and releasing it. Do this for about ten minutes.

4. **Extend your awareness and breath out into your auric field.** This may be one or more feet from your skin. You will probably notice that your auric field expands over time as you do this exercise. Breathe with your physical body and your auric field. Notice that your awareness isn't contained just inside your body.

5. **Pull your energy back into your body.** When you are finished with this exercise, pull your awareness, breath, and energy back inside your own body. Breathing with your feet will help ground you. Placing your hand over your solar plexus will pull your energy back into your body. Check where your energy is. If it's still outside your body, pull it back in with a strong intention to do so, or get up and do something physical.

Answers to Your Question

READ USING CLAIRSENTIENCE

Pair up. Get into that connected, quiet zone using whole body breathing. Before you proceed, just be with your body for a moment. Raise your hand slightly when you are connected to your body awareness to let your partner know you are ready to start the reading. Your partner should then ask a question. Without analyzing it, what is the immediate reaction of your body? Tell your partner. Discuss. (Then your partner reads your question.)

For individuals: Have your journal nearby. Use the above technique, asking your question. Journal about how your body immediately reacts without analyzing it—just make it free-form, stream of consciousness writing.

Record insights in your journal. Distance yourself from the emotions and energy of your insights. Move into your thinking mind and analyze the insights you received. What is your "gut sense" telling you about your question? If you are beginning to devise ideas for putting your psychic insights into action, take a couple of steps in your life based on this. Even little steps can create shifts in your life and give you feedback about your psychic insights.

Below is a list of the breathing exercises in other parts of the workbook that will assist with increasing your body awareness:

Breathe with Your Feet and the Earth, page 33

Crown Chakra Breathing, page 89

Extending Your Breath, pages 129-130

Occipital Lobe Breathing, page 66

Temporal Lobe Breathing, page 70

Third-Eye/Psychic Eye Breathing, page 10

Whole Body Breathing, page 104

BREATHE WITH ANY PART OF YOUR BODY.

Put your awareness deep inside an area. Suggestions follow. Be present with your breathing for a few minutes, and let that connectedness flow with your breath. As you move to each area of your body, pretend the area is the only part of you that is breathing, so that you are isolating your breath to a specific area of your body. Feel your breath move in and out of the body area. Have a talk with that area of your body if you'd like.

- Body areas: feet, hips and pelvic area, belly, breasts, brain, etc.

- Any chakra

- An area of the body you want to connect with, particularly areas you can't feel or that has experienced/ stored physical or emotional trauma

PRANAYAMA/BREATHING TECHNIQUES.

The following books have helpful exercises to improve your breathing. Along with this comes increased psychic awareness.

- *Spinal Breathing Pranayama: Journey to Inner Space,* by Yogani, 2006

- *Ways to Better Breathing,* by Carola Speads

- *Science of Breath: A Complete Manual of the Oriental Breathing Philosophy of Physical, Mental, Psychic, and Spiritual Development,* by Yogi Ramacharaka, originally published in 1904

- *Psychic Breathing: Cosmic Vitality From the Air,* by Robert Crookall, 1979

GET BODYWORK REGULARLY.

Any kind of bodywork can help you connect with your body. But energywork is particularly beneficial in sensing your body's energy, emotions, and insights. Look for energy workers who use intuitive skills in their work. Give yourself energywork, too, like Reiki. Recommended: Reiki, Therapeutic Touch, chiropractic adjustments, Cranial Sacral Therapy, Color Therapy, Aromatherapy, Acupuncture, and Reflexology.

INCREASE THE PSYCHIC SENSITIVITY IN YOUR HANDS.

This will increase your clairsentient skills for reading the energy of a person, object (as in psychometry), or any question (because questions have energy, too). "Eyeless Sight" is a technique that strengthens clairsentience. In the early 1960s, Soviet researchers studied Rosa Kuleshova, who had the ability to read words with her fingers. She initially started to develop this ability by psychically reading colors. Those who studied her ability went on to teach how to use "eyeless sight."

- *Psychic Discoveries Behind the Iron Curtain,* by Sheila Ostrander and Lynn Schroeder, *1970 & 1997*

- *Eyeless Sight,* by Jules Romains, 1978

BASIC "EYELESS SIGHT" TECHNIQUE.

Keep the focus on sensing physical characteristics—clairsentience. If you psychically see, hear, or just know the color, set that aside and return to focusing on the physical characteristics.

1. **Get colored construction paper** (cut in rectangles about the size of your hand).

   - Start with just a few colors (green, blue, red, yellow, orange).
   - After you can easily identify the first list of colors with your hands, try other colors.

2. **Put one color in front of you on the table.** Set the other colors aside.

   - Take a few deep breaths. Relax your shoulders. Slightly open your jaw at the hinge.
   - Keep your eyes open.

3. **Put your awareness inside your non-dominant hand** (or try using two fingers).

   - Put your sense of self, your focus inside your hand. It should feel like you are present inside your palm.
   - Take a moment and breathe with your palm, as if it is taking in and letting out breath. Do this for a few moments, and then let this focus relax.

4. *With eyes open*, slowly glide your non-dominant hand slightly above the colored paper.

   - **How does the color feel?** Temperature, texture, movement, emotion, etc. Be in a space of receiving instead of reaching out for something. Let sensations come to you—you won't need to go find them.
   - **Try touching the paper** with your hands, continuing to sense the characteristics of this color. Experiment with opening and closing your eyes while touching the paper.
   - **The point of this technique is to learn how to touch psychically**—to pickup physical sensations with your hand.
   - **Let go** of effort, trying, and the need to perform or achieve. By now, you probably already know that this just gets in the way of being psychic.

5. **Make notes about the characteristics of the color.** Write everything you get—whether it seems odd or it is a fleeting sensation. How you sense colors may change. My students regularly sense colors differently, so don't let your analytical mind get in the way. Some students have felt the color blue as cold, while others sense it as warm. The way *you* sense the physical characteristics of the colors is all that matters.

6. **Do this with all the colors** you initially chose until you know how each one feels. Experiment with using your dominant hand, non-dominant hand, and two fingers to see which is more psychically sensitive.

EXERCISE TO INCREASE CLAIRSENTIENCE ("EYELESS SIGHT"):

1. *With your eyes closed*, **mix up the colors.**

2. **Without looking, select one color:**

   - Put this one card in front of you on a table.
   - Put the other cards far enough away from you, so that you don't confuse them with the one you are reading.

3. **Put your awareness inside your hand.** Breathe with your hand (or palm or two fingers). Then relax your breath.

4. **Sense the color with your hand.** Let the physical characteristics of the color come towards you. If you find it helpful, hold the card.

5. **Based on what you have already learned about the colors, what color is it?** Open your eyes to see what color it is.

   - If you didn't get the color, laugh it off. Competition and anxiety get in the way of using the psychic sense.

6. **Continue with the other colors.** Mix up the color cards, selecting one card at a time, and psychically reading the physical characteristics with your hand.

7. **Take the colors with you as you go about your day.** Play with sensing them when convenient.

8. **Practice "eyeless sight" regularly:**

   • Use the same colors until you can easily sense each color and are familiar with the colors' energy and characteristics.

   • You will eventually move quickly through the steps.

   • Then, move on to the advanced techniques.

Advanced Techniques:

• **Select additional solid colors.** Get unique color swatches from the paint store.

• **Try reading textured paper** and patterned colors.

• **Type the letters of the alphabet** on white sheets of paper, with one letter on each piece. Enlarge each letter and bold the letter. Using "Eyeless Sight," see if you can read a letter with your hand or fingers using clairsentience (and without using other "clairs").

• Ask a friend to blindfold you and lead you into a room you have never been in. With your hands, read the colors, textures, and objects/people in the room without touching.

Game to Increase Clairsentience:

PSYCHIC GO FISH

This game is for two or more players, but you can also play by yourself.

Make a set of 16 cards: Create a word processing document making one entire page blue and the second page, red. Print on heavy white paper so you can't see the colors from the back side. Cut into squares. Or use colored construction paper, and tape squares on to heavy white paper (glue makes the colors bleed).

How to Play: Use clairsentience only, feeling the physical characteristics of the colors. You can also play this game using the other "clairs," so that you strengthen all the components of your psychic sense.

Mix the cards so no one knows the colors. Lay out the cards face down so they aren't touching. One person goes first by selecting one card. Turn it up, so the color is showing. Sense the color with your hand to remind yourself how that particular color feels.

Put your hand slightly above the faced-down cards, *looking for a match based on the physical sensations you know that particular color has.* Select a card. If it matches, you have a pair, and you can set the pair beside you and continue until you don't make a match. The next person goes when a match is not made. Mix the cards before the next person goes.

What was your experience?

_____

_____

_____

_____

_____

_____

_____

_____

_____

_____

TIP FOR GROUNDING: Before you do the next exercise, send a cord from your sacrum (end of spine) deep into the center of the Earth. Tell yourself you are grounded as you do the following reading.

Answers to Your Question

READ USING CLAIRSENTIENCE (PSYCHOMETRY)

Use psychometry to read an object that has personal significance to the person you are reading. Psychometry is based on the theory that an object that has meaning to its owner will carry that person's energy. Holding the object can be a helpful way of tuning into the owner. Psychometry is a useful tool for focusing your mind during a psychic reading. You might try using this technique when you are stuck or your psychic insights are all over the place. Traditionally, psychometry has been used by a psychic to tune into a missing person and to connect psychically with a loved one who has died.

In this exercise, you will be holding a personal object that belongs to the person you are reading. This can be anything, such as a special piece of jewelry that is worn regularly, or ask for a person's keys, as these carry the owner's energy. Some psychics say that using a metal object like keys, a watch, or jewelry is a better carrier of energy and so makes psychometry easier to do.

Pair up. Get into that connected, quiet zone. Hold the object in your non-dominant hand. Breathe with your whole body for a few minutes. Then move your body/energy awareness into the object. Be patient, waiting until you begin to sense the aliveness of the object. Maybe it will breathe, too—if so, synchronize your breath with the object. (Hint: Try pretending the object is breathing.)

When you are ready, tell your partner to ask a question. Allow images, thoughts, words, and feelings to come to you. Use all your "clairs." Share everything you get with your partner. Discuss.

For individuals: Put your car keys or other personal object in your non-dominant hand. Use the above instructions to connect with your body and then the object. When you sense that you are in the zone and present with the object, ask your question. Note anything you get without analyzing or thinking about it. Just let whatever comes flow from your connection with the object.

Record insights in your journal. Are you beginning to see a pattern in the answers to your question? It's okay if you aren't—just think about it and write about your insights in the journal. You are getting in the habit of looking for both psychic and analytical answers to your question, and that makes for a stronger psychic sense.

TIP FOR DISCONNECTING: After doing the foregoing exercise, wash your hands. Take a longer time soaping up and rinsing. As you do this, imagine that anything you picked up by holding the object is released from you and going down the sink pipe.

3 Play Outside Your Rut

SHIFT YOUR BRAIN

> I was driving back from a mall one night, when I got a hunch not to take my usual exit off the highway. But my conscious mind complained that going down the highway to the next exit would take me too much time, and I didn't feel like losing that time. So, I got off the exit I always take. About three miles up the road, I was stopped.
>
> Ugh! I should have listened to my hunch about taking the next exit. In front of me was a long line of cars going through a DUI checkpoint. I wasn't concerned about the DUI stop because I hadn't been drinking. But I didn't like the extra time it took me to get home! Who would have thought they would be doing a DUI check there—my rational mind couldn't conceive what my psychic mind knew.

I'd be willing to bet that all human beings have had at least one hunch. It's in our nature to have hunches. Unfortunately, our society teaches us to ignore them. Even professional psychics don't always follow their hunches, like my drive back home from the mall! When we get in a rut, we may be less likely to be aware of our hunches and to act on them.

I think subtle messages are always being picked up by our expanded awareness or extra-sensory perception, giving us additional information for dealing with life circumstances. But our conscious mind has a stronger hold on us, so the hunches are either ignored or, more often, don't get through the noise of our analytical thinking. If you want to develop your psychic sense, you need to get out of the rut that you are in. It's not just about listening to your hunches. I'm recommending you become more aware in general. And playing outside your rut can help you do that.

Most of us go through our day fixed on what is "important," and we miss other ways of perceiving that might offer helpful insights. We follow unconscious patterns. For example, we typically take the same route to work, park in the same area, and walk in one particular direction. Children (who are more easily psychic than adults) usually vary their actions. Play with changing your routine. This helps free the mind to consider other possible sources of input—like your psychic sense.

Suggestions for Playing Outside Your Rut:

SMILE TODAY.

For one day, play with smiling at people for no particular reason. Smile when you are by yourself, too. It's okay if you fake your smile. Notice how it feels in your body to smile more often.

Students get this for pre-work (homework to do before class), and they comment how smiling shifted their day. Some students said that people in their lives reacted to them differently—it was an easier day when they smiled. But that's not why I asked them to smile. I wanted them to get outside their usual routines. Smiling, particularly to yourself, is like taking a vacation. This makes room for subtle intuitions to be heard by you.

HUM TODAY.

Make up your own song as you go through your day, and hum it. Or hum a song you know. Just hum today. Can you feel the hum vibrating your pineal gland (third-eye)?

Do you remember humming as a kid? I did it a lot, more than as an adult when I learned self-limiting social rules about controlling my behavior. Humming shifts you—particularly when you make it up. It gets you in a space where you can more easily access the imagination and the psychic sense.

DRIVE A DIFFERENT ROUTE.

Whether walking or driving, go a different way than usual. Notice the feelings in your body and mind when you do this. When you recognize a difference in feeling, think about how being psychic may feel this way at first. Tell yourself that at some point you will feel comfortable being psychic.

I love to walk, and I regularly have a route that I take. One day, I decided to go in the opposite direction. It felt weird. My body knew the "right" way, and it was surprised. Psychic insights often come as surprises. Get out of your rut so you can be surprised!

BREACHING EXPERIMENT.

When I was in graduate school, I learned about breaching experiments. They are a way to make visible the social rules in our culture. You do something out of the norm, and then see how people react. Examples: Stand facing people in the elevator with your back to the door. Stand too close to a person you are talking with. Shake someone's hand longer than is socially appropriate.

This is a way for you to become aware of how you participate in the world unconsciously. Yeah, I get it that sociologists are doing these experiments to analyze how other people respond. But I'm suggesting you do this for your own education. How do you feel when you are doing a breaching experiment? What's going on in your body and mind?

This experiment can make other people uncomfortable. So, it's not a time to be mean or insulting or do something that can get you into trouble. It's a learning experiment for YOU. So make it simple and kind.

SHIFT WHERE YOU FOCUS YOUR EYES.

When we look at a television show or a speaker, we usually have our eyes focused in one obvious spot—where the action is. Try shifting your eyes and focus on what's going on behind the obvious spot or to the side of the obvious spot. Keep your focus there for ten or more seconds before you look elsewhere. The reason I'm telling you to stay there for ten-plus seconds is that you will probably shift your eyes more quickly because you have been taught it's not important to look at these areas.

When I started doing readings, I had no one to tell me what to do. I naturally shifted my eyes to my left in the space near the person's right shoulder. Sure, I would glance back to my client's eyes at times. But I read better when I'm not connecting socially to a person by looking them in the eyes. When I see clients in person, and they are from the South (it's the accent or their mannerisms), I usually apologize and explain why I'm not looking at them. I'm from the South where it's considered polite to look one in the eyes when talking to one another. At the urging of a client, I started doing readings via Skype. And I hated it. I felt like I needed to look at my client more often because there was no personal, body connection like there was with someone who was in the same room with me. I'm at my best doing phone readings, because I can ignore social niceties almost completely and focus on being psychic!

So shift your eye focus as an exercise in allowing other input to enter into your awareness.

USE YOUR NON-DOMINANT HAND.

Do this for things for which you would normally use your dominant hand. Each time you remember to do this, think about how you are strengthening your psychic sense.

I was a teen when my friends and I starting having fun writing with our left hands—most of us were right-handed. Some think we access the creative, right brain by doing this. The point of using your non-dominant hand is to get out of your rut, to think differently, to act in the world differently. It's all done to shake us out of the normalcy and let something psychic enter into our awareness.

WASH YOUR HANDS.

After tentatively making a decision (even minor ones, like what to eat for lunch), get up and wash your hands. Return to the decision and see if you view it differently.

I started washing my hands as a way to disconnect after giving a massage, and I've found it a useful way to shift myself ever since. Intense focusing until you get something done is an analytical brain activity. When students are stuck during class, I sometimes ask them to get up and wash their hands. It can release them from being stuck.

CLOUD BUSTING.

On a day with puffy clouds, lie on the ground and look up into the sky. Find shapes of animals, faces, and other designs. Connect with a cloud by putting your awareness with it. Invite the cloud to move or disperse. Resist trying; allow.

I did this as a kid all the time, and I bet you did, too. My sister and I would lie on the ground and gaze at the clouds, talking about the animals we saw. It was a wonderful way to spend an afternoon. I'll tell you a secret. I still look at the clouds and see funny characters that I imagine doing all sorts of wonderful things, while I'm down here on Earth stuck doing mundane things.

CALL SOMEONE UNEXPECTEDLY.

Is there a friend, family member, or other person you haven't called in a while? If so, call that person today for no special reason other than to say hello; just call for the heck of it.

I'm not necessarily referring to those times when you get a hunch to call someone, only to discover they were thinking of you or needed to talk. The suggestion here is to consciously decide to get out of your rut and make a call.

PERFORM RANDOM ACTS OF KINDNESS.

Pick one day a month to do random acts of kindness. Some examples: Return someone's grocery cart for them. Hold the door open for someone, while smiling (I know what you are thinking—this used to be part of normal civility). For ideas, go to www.RandomActsOfKindness.org

My son told me about a time he went to the McDonald's drive-through for breakfast. When he got to the window to pay, he was told that the person in the car ahead of him had paid for his meal. That touched him. I could hear it in his voice as he told me about it. For the rest of his day, he thought about that unexpected thoughtfulness. It led him to do the same for others. It shifted him out of his rut.

Exercise to Play Outside Your Rut

WALK BACKWARDS.

(Do not do this by yourself)

Pair up. One person does the exercise while the other "spots"—to be sure the person is safe and supported. Leave your eyes open or closed; you decide. Put your awareness with your entire back. Make sure you have this connection before proceeding. Walk backwards, using your clairsentient awareness in your back to direct you. Notice how your back can sense and "see" how to best move "forward." The spotter assists if needed, preventing the person from walking into something or falling.

What was your experience?

_____

_____

_____

_____

_____

_____

_____

_____

_____

_____

_____

_____

_____

Create Your Package!

TIP FOR GOOD ETHICS: Refrain from psychic gossip: this would be using your abilities to gain an advantage over someone else or to snoop.

Answers to Your Question

READ BY PLAYING OUTSIDE YOUR RUT

Write your question on a piece of paper, and put it in your pocket, or post the question on your cell phone. As you go about your day, look at your question. Then smile at the question, or try humming to your question, as if it were a person. Do this several times a day.

Note anything you get without analyzing or thinking about it. Don't underestimate that doing little things outside of your routine can give you psychic insights. It's our thinking, trying mind that works hard to get insights. The psychic mind is more subtle, so try just smiling and humming.

Record insights in your journal. Write about how it felt to "play outside your rut." This is a fun way to develop your psychic abilities—so enjoy writing your thoughts about this exercise. Were you able to get outside your rut to get answers to your question? Is there one small, out-of-the-ordinary step you can take to act outside your rut based on your insights? Little steps outside our ruts can bring new life experiences!

4 Dreams

GUIDANCE AS YOU SLEEP

Dreams have always been a significant part of my psychic ability. The first dream I remember having was when I was six years old. For years, as a child, I spent many nights traveling outside my body, exploring other worlds. I looked forward to going to bed at night because I so enjoyed my dream travels. But at 19, my joy of dreaming would shake my world and push me on a journey to strengthen my psychic abilities.

For almost three months, I regularly had a recurring dream of being attacked near my home. During my waking hours, if I stared off into nothingness (something I have always done a great deal), the vision of being attacked came forward into my awareness. Then the dreams stopped, and for two weeks I wasn't plagued by fear. But that didn't last.

Two weeks after my nightmares stopped, I was attacked in just about the same way as in my dreams. The only difference was that it was daytime in my dreams, but the actual attack happened at night.

I walked past some bushes across the street from where my husband and neighbors were standing. Although I didn't hear a thing, I immediately ran, knowing I needed to run. I must have been screaming because people who lived several apartment buildings away later told me they had heard my terrified screams.

A man had come from behind the bushes and ran after me. He took hold of me, and I bent over—all action coming from instinct. I knew nothing of what was happening. My hands must have been around my neck because there would be cuts on the outsides of my hands where he put a wire around my neck. I needed eight stitches that people today mistakenly assume are the scars left from thyroid surgery.

I think my dreams saved me. Perhaps I was rehearsing this soon-to-be experience so I would survive. I don't know why I had my hands near my neck. He was in charge, so he could have easily and quickly pulled that wire around me. My husband and others came running. He never tried to do anything but yank that wire around my neck. But I had my hands there. Why? I think because my dreams prepared me.

I had had psychic dreams before that terrifying experience. My dreams had often told me what was going to happen in my life. But I didn't listen. This time, I wasn't about to allow something so horrible to happen again! I threw myself into learning about dreams. I wrote five to seven dreams in my journal just about every night—which is about all the dreams we have each night. I could remember dreams all day long, and put them in my journal after work. I learned how to interpret dreams, attended dream conferences, and joined dream groups. As I said earlier, I was never going to let this happen to me again. Looking back, I couldn't know, at the age of nine when my psychic dreaming had started, what to do with these dreams. But at 19, I was determined that I would get every bit of guidance from my dreams so something frightening would never, ever come down on me again!

One of the very best sources of psychic information is in your dreams. In my experience teaching dream classes, leading dream groups, and following my own dreams for over forty years, I know we dream about our futures. We have several dreams about major life events before they happen—events that affect our personal lives as well as the world. In a sense, all dreams are psychic because they come from expanded awareness, and they give us helpful insights about our life.

If you want to develop your psychic abilities, learning how to recall and make sense of your dreams is important. As you move through some of the stuff locked away in your unconscious mind, your dreams will be clearer and easier to understand. You will likely discover that you remember more psychic dreams with helpful information. Your psychic abilities during your waking hours will also be strengthened by doing dreamwork.

At some point, I moved past thinking that I had to remember and work with every dream, so that I could prevent problems. I didn't want that kind of panicked approach to life. Focusing on your dreams, as well as having strong psychic abilities, shouldn't be about controlling your life so bad things don't happen. Part of life is learning to deal with problems—not eliminate them, even if that were possible.

The benefits of working with dreams:

1. Assist in solving problems.
2. Give input for making decisions.
3. Transform attitudes and emotions.
4. Provide insights for resolving interpersonal conflicts.
5. Get guidance about current or unknown physical problems.
6. Experience healing within the dream.
7. Provide access to the realm of ideas and inventions.
8. Provide a resource for creativity.
9. Preview significant future life events, including world events.
10. Provide an opportunity for communication with friends, loved ones, and others (both here and in spirit).
11. Develop the psychic sense.
12. Expand spiritual awareness, a greater connection with what lies beyond the individual, the transpersonal.
13. Offer travel to other realms of being.
14. Provide access to the mystical unknown.

Interpretation Technique

TITLE YOUR DREAM

If you have limited time to work with a dream, this technique is quick.

1. **Title.** Give your dream a meaningful title.

2. **Reflection.** How does this title reflect happenings in your life?

3. **Contemplate.** Mull over the title for the rest of the day to discover other possible ways to understand the dream.

4. **Understanding of the Dream.** What do you think the dream might be telling you?

5. **Action.** What steps do you want to take based upon the understanding you reached about the dream?

EXAMPLE:

Dream: I stand in my living room as someone tries to open my front door. I'm afraid. A man looks in and sees that I am there and then closes the door without ever showing his face. Then I see the door open from the garage to the kitchen. I still cannot move. A man walks in and looks around, ignoring me. I am afraid.

1. **Title:**

"I'm Being Invaded" or "I Freeze When Invaded"

2. **How Title Reflects My Life:**

I am feeling invaded and ignored by my husband.

3. **Insight from Contemplation:**

After mulling it over, I am struck that I didn't do anything in the dream when I was being invaded and ignored. After all, someone has broken into my house (broken into me), and I'm just standing there! What does this say about me—that I allow people to invade me?

4. **Understanding of Dream:**

Maybe the dream is reflecting my marriage—but more importantly, that I'm not taking good care of myself—that maybe I don't take good care of myself in relationships.

5. **Action:**

Maybe the first step is just to recognize what I feel and how I react in relation to my husband. I plan to write about the time yesterday when he and I had an argument. Maybe I should consider getting some therapy.

EXERCISE:

Get a dream from your journal. It can be a current one or a dream you had long ago. Interpreting older dreams can also give you helpful insight.

Read the dream and give it a meaningful title.

Over the next day, think about the title, not the dream, exploring how the title speaks to your life. Write about your insights in your journal, including possible steps you might take.

Tips for Remembering Dreams

FOCUS ON DREAMING:

1. **Develop an interest in dreams.** Read books on dreams, take dream courses, join dream study groups, and talk with your friends about your dreams and your interest in dreaming. Throughout the day, affirm that you will recall your dreams by saying to yourself, "I remember my dreams."

2. **Why do you want to remember your dreams?** Write in your journal your reasons for wanting to work with dreams. This sends a message to your dreaming mind that you are interested in getting insights from your dreams.

3. **Take action on your dreams.** The meaning of a dream comes from actualizing it, rather than just interpreting it intellectually—put the dream into action; do something with it. Recall and quality of your dreams will be enhanced as you put your interpretation into action. Every dream does not, however, need to be interpreted and acted on. Do not feel you will be missing something if you choose not to work with or remember every dream.

4. **Use hypnosis to bring greater attention to your dreams.** See www.HealthJourneys.com for a variety of hypnosis recordings.

DO YOUR INNER WORK:

5. **Include self-awareness techniques in your life.**
   Be open to exploring your inner world using tools such as the following:

   Psychotherapy. Seek professional help in healing childhood issues and for coming into greater awareness of your emotions.

   Hypnosis. This helps to remove the energetic triggers that lie in the unconscious mind that continue to influence your life. You can also use professional hypnosis or self-hypnosis to re-enter a dream to explore its significance to your life.

   Bodywork. Your body has wisdom. Receiving bodywork from a professional trained in holistic touch, particularly energywork, can assist in listening to your body.

   Journal writing. Write about your thoughts, frustrations, problems, joys, decisions, and life events in a journal. This is perhaps the best tool for staying in contact with your inner self. You will also find that as you write, you will receive inspirations and insights into your life. This comes from the same mind space as your dreams.

   Small group work. Participating in small groups contributes to personal growth. The groups can be for therapy, dreamwork, or any group where people come together to explore their inner world. Small groups are seedbeds for enhanced consciousness, because in the process of the exchange, we come into greater awareness about ourselves and our place in the world.

   Meditation. Your dreams come from your expanded awareness, therefore, attunement to this part of yourself can facilitate the recall of dreams.

6. **Spend quiet alone time each day.**
   It's difficult to hear your inner voice when there is a lot of noise in your life. How often is there noise in your life? Recognizing that is the first step to putting silence in your life. Turn off the television and the radio, silence electronic devices, and remove other noises. Try driving in the car without the radio on. Spend some time each day alone, without reading a book or doing anything and without noise of any kind (not even soothing music).

   Even if you don't hear your inner voice during quiet times, you are more likely to hear it at other times because you have quiet spaces in your day. Quiet alone-time is particularly helpful before going to bed because it creates a space and a willingness on your part to listen to your inner voice through your dreams.

This alone-time could include meditation. But what is being described here is more of a time of contemplation, an allowing of the inner voice to speak to you; an active meditation (not one where you block out all thoughts, but one where you welcome inspiration and new ideas from your inner voice).

BEFORE YOU GO TO BED:

7. Review your journal.

It can include your dreams, interpretations, and your life concerns. Write in your journal before going to sleep. Review your dreams from previous nights. This brings focus to your dreams before entering into sleep.

8. Place paper, pencil, and light by the bed.

Record your dreams immediately upon waking. You can also use a recording device.

9. Use a pre-sleep hypnotic suggestion.

While entering sleep, repeat a suggestion, such as, "I remember my dreams when I awake." You can also use a pre-sleep suggestion to help you with a current problem, "Tonight, I will dream about (state the problem/concern)."

To increase your psychic abilities, ask silently over and over as you enter into sleep: "Am I psychic?" The unconscious mind wants to answer yes/no questions, and your dreams will give you a lot more than a simple yes/no.

10. Don't move upon waking.

Keep your eyes closed. Allow your mind to review the night's dreams. Slowly move your body as you get your paper and pen, and write dreams in an outline format. Fill in the details now if you have time, or do it later. You will also find it helpful to wake up before the alarm, as the sound may hinder dream recall.

11. Write down something, anything!

Whether it is a few words, one sentence, or just how you felt upon waking, write something about your nighttime sleep. Consistency in dreamwork brings improved results.

TAKE IT EASY:

12. Take a relaxing vacation.

Most people tend to remember more and clearer dreams while on vacation. This is probably because we have less or different stresses.

13. Let yourself fail.

Anxiety over trying to remember dreams can diminish dream recall.

Interpretation Technique

DREAM PICTURES

1. Paint or sketch pictures of your dreams.

For two weeks, make pictures of your dreams instead of analyzing or interpreting them with your thinking mind. Use watercolors, crayons, colored pencils, and other art material. Create a single picture that represents your dream, not a series of cartoon frames. Art ability isn't important. The picture can be a detailed sketch of a specific part of your dream or an abstract expression of how your dream makes you feel.

2. After you have about ten pictures, lay them out on the floor, a large table, or a bed.

You could also tape them to a wall. Stand back and take in the entirety of the pictures instead of looking at each one individually. What are your first, immediate reactions to what you see? Let your body and emotions respond to the pictures, giving your analytical mind a rest. Take it all in, and allow insights to come to you about what's happening in the pictures.

Now turn to your analytical mind, and consider what's going on in the pictures. Assess them individually, collectively, and make connections between two or more pictures. What do you think your dreaming mind is trying to tell you?

If you'd like, ask trusted family and friends to give input on what they see happening in the pictures, without telling them they represent dreams. They may try to figure out what the dreams are, and that's not the point.

3. **Write in your dream journal about the insights you received.**

   What steps might you take in your life based on the insights? When you value your dreams by incorporating them in your life in some way, your dreams and your psychic sense get stronger.

4. **Over time you may see patterns in your dream pictures.**

   When you look back at your dream pictures after some time has passed, you may be surprised at what you can see in them.

EXERCISE:

Gather the ten-plus pictures that you have been creating since earlier in the workbook. Use the above interpretation technique to explore the significance of the dreams. Write in your journal about the insights you received.

On the next few nights after working with the pictures, pay special attention to your dreams. This exercise has taken several weeks to complete, and the focus you have given to your dreams should provide you with increased dream recall and better quality messages.

Create Your Package!

TIP FOR GOOD DISCONNECTING:	How is your body feeling right now?
	Brush down your body. With long sweeps of your hand, brush down your arms, head, neck, trunk, hips, and legs/feet.
	How does your body feel now?

Basics of Dream Interpretation

1. **You are the best interpreter of your dreams.**

   When assisting others to understand their dreams, use the approach of a facilitator that offers suggestions, instead of being an expert with a know-it-all attitude. For example, you can offer your perspective of someone's dream based on what it might mean if *you* had the dream. When giving input, preface your comments with, "If it were my dream…" Another facilitator approach is to ask questions, such as, "In your dream, you are going down a long and winding road. Are you experiencing something in your life that is taking a long time and that has twists and turns, like a winding road?"

You, the dreamer, are the best interpreter because:

- You are the one who needs to act on the dream, and you may not feel responsible for this, if someone else does the interpretation.

- The symbols are yours and not another person's; only you can ultimately give them meaning.

- You grow and unfold in consciousness when you grapple with understanding your dream's images and symbols.

2. **If you are working in a group, respect the privacy of group members.**
   Do not discuss group members' dream content and interpretation outside the group. During the group, share only that personal information you feel comfortable sharing. Do not pressure others to give personal information.

3. **Dreams can have multiple interpretations.**
   Be open to several possible meanings. We operate on many different levels, and this is reflected in our dreams. Remain open to further insights about a dream while integrating your interpretations into your life.

4. **All dreams do not need to be interpreted.**
   Our dreams influence our lives just by having them.

5. **Dreams exist outside of time and space.**
   Dreams can have relevancy to your life regardless of when you had them. Go back through your journal, and select dreams to work on like those from your childhood and particularly recurring dreams.

6. **Interpret dreams by acting on them.**
   Dreams become more helpful when you find a way to integrate them into your life in some way. Not all dreams require specific action; the point is to value your dreams by using the insights you gain from them. The idea to interpret dreams by acting on them came from the Edgar Cayce material.

Exercise to Increase Psychic Dreaming Skills:

SCHEDULE A DREAM MEET-UP

Get a friend to join you in this experience. Agree on a specific place that exists in waking reality, where you both will meet-up during your dreams. As you enter into sleep, think about your friend and expect to meet her/him at the location.

When you wake up in the morning, record your dreams, even if you don't think you made it to the agreed-upon place or saw your friend. Do this three nights in a row; then stop for one night; then do the same meet-up for two more nights. Discuss your dreams with your friend each day.

For individuals: Instead of meeting up with a friend in our world, use this exercise to connect with a spirit, guide, or loved one in spirit.

What was your experience?

_____

_____

_____

_____

_____

_____

_____

_____

_____

_____

_____

_____

_____

Psychic Dreaming

Below are suggestions for increasing the quality and number of psychic insights.

SET THE INTENTION TO HAVE PSYCHIC DREAMS

1. **Third-Eye (Psychic Eye) Breathing.**

    Do this throughout your day except when driving or other times when you need to pay attention. Refer to page 10 for instructions.

    *   Say silently to yourself or out loud, "I am psychic. Tonight, I will have psychic dreams." Say this while breathing with your third-eye and while imagining that you are waking up excited that you have had a psychic dream. This affirmative statement works with the unconscious mind to open your innate psychic sense and increases the likelihood that you will have psychic dreams.

    *   Ground yourself after using this exercise by closing your third-eye (use the image of a closed door or eye), and breathe with your feet and the Earth.

2. **Re-mind yourself.**

    Set your watch, cell phone, or some other timing device to beep every hour. When you hear the beep, stop what you are doing, take a breath, and say to yourself something like, "Oh, yeah, I am having a psychic dream," or "I am having a psychic dream about _____." (Use whatever you would like to get information about, such as, "my future," "my job").

3. **As you go to sleep, breathe with your third-eye while asking (silently to yourself), "Am I having a psychic dream?"**

    Ask this question over and over until you enter into sleep. If your mind wanders, softly bring it back to the question and the third-eye breathing. The time before entering into sleep is one of the best times for trance work like this.

    When you wake up in the morning, record your dreams. Writing something every morning increases your ability to remember dreams. So if you don't recall a dream, write in your journal how you felt upon waking.

4. **Make an herbal dream pouch.**

    Get a square of muslin and a string or a small draw-string bag. Fill it with herbs that are known to assist in psychic development. Mugwort is the most commonly used herb to enhance dreams. Other herbs and spices include cloves, cinnamon, jasmine, mint, or pine. Include in the bag small stones, such as amethyst. You also can place an herbal oil just underneath your nose as well as on your third-eye. Smelling the scents while you are asleep facilitates dream recall and reminds your sleeping mind that you want helpful dreams.

HOW TO KNOW A DREAM IS PSYCHIC

1. **Get in the habit of reviewing your journal.**

    One of the best ways to understand your own unique way of dreaming psychically is to keep a journal and review the past six months to a year. You are more likely to see trends about where your life is going with this look back. Future life events are revealed in a series of dreams over months to years before the events happen. So, if you regularly review past dreams, you will begin to understand what your dreams are telling you about your future.

2. **When working with a dream, always consider the possibility it may be psychic.**

    *   **Be alert for psychic information** by asking yourself, "If this dream were telepathic, what would it be telling me?" or "If this were a warning dream, what might it be warning me of?" or "If this is a precognitive dream, what might it be showing me about my future?"

    *   **Record synchronicities.** Synchronicity is a meaningful coincidence that has no apparent cause and effect. Use a small notebook to record synchronistic moments that happen throughout your day. You can also include psychic hunches. Being aware of how synchronicity plays out in your life connects you to the flow of energy of which dreams are a part. This exercise can help you make connections between your waking and dreaming experiences.

Psychic dream readings.

This method was developed by Robin A. Carter, who presented the paper "Dreaming to Help Others," at the Annual Conference of the Association for the Study of Dreams, in Washington, D.C., in June 1987. I happened to be sitting next to her and we struck up a conversation about her research. I had always had psychic dreams, but this was the first time I realized that I could intentionally setup my dreams to give a psychic reading. Robin based her research on Henry Reed's "Dream Helper Ceremony" (see *Getting Help from Your Dreams*, by Henry Reed, 1988). Here is the procedure:

- **Recruit a volunteer.** It is better to get a volunteer you don't know. Explain to the person that you would like to see if you could get helpful information for her (or him) by having dreams for her. The volunteer doesn't have to believe in the helpfulness of dreams.

- **Ask the volunteer to think of a problem or issue she needs help with.** The volunteer does not give you any information about herself or the problem/issue.

- **Ask the volunteer to loan you a personal item.** This should be something small because you will be putting it underneath your pillow. It should be particularly meaningful to her or something she's worn regularly, like a watch.

- **Ask the volunteer to meditate or share a silent moment with you.** Do whatever the volunteer feels comfortable with. The volunteer doesn't need to meet with you face-to-face.

- **Tell the volunteer that you will be dreaming a solution to her problem/issue.** Set aside one to three consecutive nights for dreaming for the volunteer. On the subsequent nights, when you are not focusing on the volunteer, your dreams might offer additional insights. Sometimes when we ease up on the desire to have dreams, they will flow more readily.

- **On the night you dream for the volunteer:** Meditate and send energy to the volunteer and her problem/issue. At bedtime, hold the volunteer's personal item in your hands as you do the following:

Affirm you are dreaming only for the volunteer:
"I dream tonight only for .... (name of volunteer)."

Give up dreaming for yourself that night:
"I release my dreams tonight for my life, so that I may be a channel of service to .... (name of volunteer)."

Affirm you will remember your dreams:
"I remember my dreams when I wake up."

As you touch the personal item, say:
"This is a physical reminder that I am dreaming for .... (name of volunteer) tonight."

If you wake up during the night, affirm that you are dreaming for the volunteer:
"I am dreaming for .... (name of volunteer)."

As you enter into sleep, think about the person you are dreaming for. Visualize her being with you and holding her personal object. Breathe with this image, expecting to have helpful dreams for her tonight. Do this as you enter into sleep. (The breathing technique is my addition to Robin's protocol.)

- **Record your dreams.** Include all details, even if they seem to relate to you or to people you know.

- **Interpret the dreams,** understanding that interpretation using this procedure is ultimately a process between you and the volunteer.

- **Meet with the volunteer.** You can do this through email or phone. Give the volunteer copies of all your dreams and your initial interpretations, even if you think the dreams are not about the volunteer. Discuss your interpretation of how the dreams may apply to the volunteer. Ask the volunteer what the dreams mean to her. Be respectful because the volunteer may not want to divulge personal information to you and may be surprised that you so intimately "read" private information through your dreams.

Answers to Your Question
GET A HELPFUL DREAM

Write your question on a piece of paper and put it under your pillow. As you go to sleep, put your energy awareness with your question, and breathe with it. Silently ask your question over and over until you enter into sleep. If your mind wanders, softly bring it back to the question.

When you wake up in the morning, record your dreams or how you felt upon waking if you didn't recall a dream.

Record insights in your journal. Use one or more of the dream interpretation techniques to work with your dream. Create a tentative list of steps you might take based on your assessment of the dream's meaning. Then take a step. Your psychic abilities, like your dreams, get stronger when you act on them!

Interpretation Technique
CREATE YOUR OWN DREAM DICTIONARY

1. **Circle the main symbols and whatever you feel drawn to** as you read the dream, *e.g.*, objects and characters, such as furniture, vehicles, animals, and people.
2. **Give a brief definition (1 to 3 words) for each symbol.** The definition is what it means to you and not an interpretation from a dream dictionary. The definitions are often simple and obvious.
3. **Rewrite your dream,** replacing the definitions in step 2.
4. What meaning do you get from the new dream?
5. What action or changes do you want to make based on this dream?

EXAMPLE

Dream: I come into my office one morning and everything has been rearranged. My desk is gone, but I have a new one. Al walks into my office. I haven't seen him for a long time. He tells me that all the file cabinets were put out in the center of the mall. He grabbed me two new ones. My old ones had black marks on them.

1. Main Symbols:

Office, Desk, Al, File Cabinets, Mall

2. Brief Definition:

Office = where I work

Desk = what I work on

Al = partner I had when I no longer had a job

File Cabinets = material I use to do my job

Mall = where I do my shopping

3. Rewritten Dream:

I come into *the place where I work* one morning and everything has been rearranged. *What I work on* is gone, but I have a new one. *I no longer have a job* walks into my office. I haven't seen *no longer have a job* for a long time. He tells me that all the *material I used to do my job* was put out in the center of *where I do my shopping*. He grabbed me two new *materials I use to do my job*. My old *materials I use to do my job* were old with black marks.

4. Understanding of Dream:

The dream seems to be suggesting that I might lose my job. The dream is also suggesting that the job I have now isn't all that great and that I will get new and better work. Maybe I have been blacklisted (black marks).

5. Action:

I will consider the possibility that I might lose my job. I also will examine what I like and dislike about my job and what kind of work I would rather be doing. I will be open to future dreams about the possibility that I might lose my job, knowing that my dreams will provide me with alternatives.

Three months after having this dream, I lost my job.

EXERCISE:

Use the above technique to interpret a dream. Write about your insights in your journal, including possible steps you might take.

CHECK OUT THESE WEBSITES:

Association for the Study of Dreams
www.asdreams.org/

Stanley Krippner, Ph.D.
http://stanleykrippner.weebly.com//

Robert Moss
www.mossdreams.com

Henry Reed, Ph.D.
www.creativespirit.net/henryreed/

Interpretation Technique

TURNING YOUR DREAM INTO QUESTIONS

1. **Turn the dream process (what's happening in the dream) into questions.**
    Start at the beginning of your dream, and select a sentence or section of the dream. Turn this into a question. Does it apply to your life in some way? Continue through the dream, turning everything (the symbols, happenings, and feelings) into questions about your life.

2. **Understanding of Dream.**
    What do you think the dream might be telling you?

3. **Action.**
    What steps do you want to take based upon the understanding you reached about the dream?

EXAMPLE

Dream: I am in my car with two other people. We are going to take a big exam. But when we get to the parking lot, there is a security guard who won't let us enter, because he says we don't have enough people with us in the car to get a parking space. We can see that there are plenty of spaces. I decide to enter a different way.

1. **Questions:**
    Are you doing something with two other people?

    Are you currently involved in a big life event, a big exam, a big test of yourself; something you have to pass to get what you want?

    Is somebody not letting you do something?

    Is there a person who is controlling your access to something?

    Do you have people on your side, but not enough to get what you want?

    Is there another way to get what you want?

2. **Understanding of Dream:**
    As I answered the questions, I thought my dream reflected a work problem I was having with some powerful people. I don't have enough people on my side.

3. **Action:**
    If I want to resolve this work problem, I will need different approaches and strategies other than those I am currently using. Maybe a more indirect way will work to resolve the issue. I've got colleagues who will help me with this, and I plan to discuss this with them.

EXERCISE:

Use the above technique to interpret a dream. Write about your insights in your journal, including possible steps you might take.

To gain experience with this technique, ask a friend if she/he will go through your dream, using this technique to ask you questions that may apply to your life. You might also do this for your friend's dream.

_____

_____

_____

_____

_____

_____

_____

_____

_____

_____

_____

Create Your Package!

TIP FOR GROUNDING:
Play with being invisible.

Sense the energy around your body,

and then pull it in closer to yourself.

Or, put on a Harry Potter "invisibility cloak."

Notice how people relate to you.

5 Creativity
USE YOUR IMAGINATION—IT'S PSYCHIC!

It is sixth grade, and I am walking into French class. I look longingly up the hall to the kids walking into art class, wishing I could go to their class instead of mine. But I don't have any art talent. Besides, I'm expected to take a language class to prepare for college. Those kids seem to have more fun than me. Sometimes, I get to peek into the room and see all kinds of wonderful colors and paintings and weird-looking sculptures.

I just assumed I couldn't take art because I had no talent. Those kids in the fun room seemed to already have art ability—it came naturally to them. And although I didn't think I would be allowed to take the class because I had no talent—even if I was allowed—I didn't want to be embarrassed. Those kids were good.

Forty years later, I tell students who don't think they are good enough to be psychic that they have a natural psychic sense—everyone does. And my friend, Lisa, who teaches Aura Painting in the Aspen Program, is always telling me that doing art is a learned skill. That's just what I say about psychic development. Lisa says that anyone can learn art techniques. What makes a good artist is something in *here*. (She points to her heart.)

That's the same as you are doing now with this workbook, strengthening your psychic abilities. It's a learned skill. You are learning techniques, getting tools, and practicing your skills. But really, it's the shift you make in your mind, setting aside thinking and analyzing to allowing insights to come to you—that's what makes the best psychics!

The psychic sense is a function of the imagination. So anything that increases your imaginative or creative skills will benefit your psychic abilities. Be creative for the pure joy of it instead of doing this solely to develop your psychic abilities. Have fun!

I have done psychic readings for many creative people: dancers, actors, musicians, writers, and artists. It's a wonderful experience to do these readings. Most of them are open and easy to read because they live in that world of the creative imagination, the psychic. Over the years, I've told some clients that they have such a natural talent for the creative that I recommend they take art, writing, or other types of classes, instead of taking my psychic development program. Their psychic abilities will flower just as well.

Tools to Increase Your Creativity:

Art. Attend an art class at a local recreation center, arts and crafts store, or community education at a local college. Or buy some art materials, and create art on your own, staying away from the rules. Expand your concept of what art is—it can include so many ideas!

- **Include art in your journal.** In addition to writing, paint how you feel about life on a particular day. The paintings can be abstract or realistic, depending upon what you want to do. Be sure to date them, and maybe jot a few words on the paper. Over time, glance through your journal—what are the paintings saying about your life?

- **Finger paint!** Call up your inner child, and dip your fingers into paint, allowing fun and joy to flow on the paper.

- **Play with clay.** You don't have to be an expert to play with clay creatively. Purchase clay at hobby and craft stores. Instead of deciding what you will create, squish it in your hands and allow something to reveal itself from the clay. Remember doing that as a kid?

- **Copy an image.** Get a picture, or look at something in the room. With paper and pencil, copy it. Look at part of it and then draw a section of the picture, and then return to look at the picture, and repeat. Don't copy the image from memory. Don't add to what you see. The purpose of this exercise is to copy the picture exactly, as best you can. My artist friend, Lisa, tells me this engages your right, creative mind.

- **Doodle.** It stretches your brain and creativity. Doodling distracts your mind; gets you out of analytical thinking. Get the book, *Brain Games: Dare to Doodle* (Creative Exercises for a Healthy Noodle!).

Creative Writing. Stories tell themselves, and so does psychic information. Instead of doing an outline or planning what you are going to write, sit with the paper, and allow an idea to speak itself by writing whatever comes to mind.

- **Poetry.** Poetry writes like music, releasing feelings and ideas into a chaos of connection and meaning. Let your inner poet write you.

- **Inspirational Writing.** Start by writing about your day and life concerns. Let it flow into receiving inspiring ideas for solving life issues. Just let this kind of writing happen; let go of thinking too hard.

Creative Movement. Put on beautiful music (try the classics, waltzes, etc.) and dance. This is the time for free-form movement, so don't follow specific dance steps. Allow the music to come into your body, and let a flow of energy lead your body into movement. You aren't deciding how to dance. You are allowing the music and your body to create the dance.

Music. Learn a musical instrument, like a flute, harp, or guitar. Allow music to flow from your connection with the instrument instead of playing a specific music piece. Also include all kinds of music in your life, listening to the rhythm and beat of the music and allowing the music to take you on journeys!

- Pay attention to how music affects each chakra and its associated endocrine gland (see page 88). Some classical music tends to stimulate the third-eye and crown chakras.

CREATIVE EXERCISE:

Draw something starting with the line below. Begin by getting into that connected, quiet zone. Then be present with the line below—breathe with it; feel it. Then draw—anything—without thinking about it, without planning.

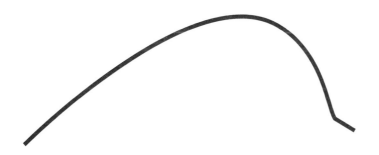

Answers to Your Question

SECONDARY IMAGERY

This method uses an art technique called "secondary imagery" to receive insights about your question. Secondary painting is based on the idea that something or someone other than you is involved in communicating messages about your question. Unexpected images will appear in the paint.

You'll need watercolor, brushes, watercolor paper, and a cup of water. Start by getting the paper wet by gliding a liberal amount of water onto the paper with the paintbrush. Then put your energy awareness with your question. From that connection select a color, and paint anything that comes to mind.

Don't think about what you want to draw. Instead, let your selection of colors and what you paint come from your energy connection with your question. Before the colors dry, pick up the paper and gently move it around, allowing paint to shift and swirl until you feel it's finished.

Images may appear in the painting without your intention. "Secondary imagery" is more likely to occur when the paint you apply is watery. When the paint dries, images may appear. Regardless of whether you use watery paint, or even crayons, you may see images come that you did not intend to draw—especially when looking at the painting over time.

Examine the painting in its various stages of drying. What do you see in the painting? You might also ask trusted friends and family members. It's sort of like looking for images in clouds. Have fun with this; be lighthearted and curious about what might reveal itself in your picture. Then later analyze your insights in relation to your question.

Record insights in your journal. Jot notes in your journal over the next few days about what you see in the painting. Don't move to analyzing what you get just yet. Be with the image for a few days. When you are finished getting insights from the secondary imagery, go over your notes and write two sentences about what you think the message is. Now what do you want to do based on this?

6 Nature Awareness

BE PRESENT WITH NATURE

I grew up in the Rosemont area of Alexandria, Virginia, near the Masonic Temple, on Russell Road, in an area with tree-lined streets. Our Dutch colonial house was built in the 1920s. Just up the street was a house from the nineteenth century. Our yard was filled with old oak trees, tulip poplars, antique roses, a huge spirea bush that I hid under, and an apple tree so old it was eventually cut down.

Behind the double-car garage that the kids in the neighborhood called the Fox Barn, were several lilac bushes, huge to a young girl. Underneath the canopy of the lilacs, I placed rocks from the yard in a horseshoe shape. I regularly sat there by myself on the Earth, sitting at the back of the U. At some point, in the silence, I would feel my body connecting with the ground, extending beyond my private sanctuary to my yard. This is the kind of thing kids did back then when TV and the Internet weren't distracting us.

Thirty years later, after my first and, so far, only sweat lodge, I re-experienced that connection with my breath and body and the Earth's breath and body. I had always wondered what a sweat lodge would be like. The heat, the steam of the rocks, the people who gathered, some I knew, others I'd just met—my body was both frightened and awed by the experience.

Just ordinary Virginia rocks that had been heated the entire day by fire were in the sweat lodge. Sage, sweetgrass, and other unknown-to-me herbs were at times thrown on the rocks—the scents filling every open pore of my skin. At times, we would come out into the cool mountain night—so many stars in the sky and we were far enough away from the city to actually see them. I remember seeing stars when I was a kid—before city lights wiped them out. What kind of world do we create when we can no longer gaze at the stars?

It was after midnight when we finished. Finally at home, I lay in my bed realizing, for the first time, that my body was trembling. As I lay there, I could feel my whole body breathing. Without any effort at all, as if it was just a natural thing for a human animal to do; I could feel every individual blade of grass breathing in my yard. We started breathing together as I entered into a deep sleep. The dreams that night were wild and life changing! I was still in graduate school completing my research and dissertation. But my body was reminding me of a different way of living and being in the world—and I craved that!

Building a relationship with Nature offers another way to develop your psychic sense—something most children do. Nature can give you psychic insights about your life and especially the environment. Think back to what you enjoyed in Nature, and start including that in your life again. Following are some exercises to consider incorporating into your daily living.

MAKING CONNECTIONS WITH YOUR ENERGY AND BREATH AWARENESS

Use this technique to make a connection to whatever you want to read:
a person, a question, a time in the future, and more. You can do this at any place,
but for this exercise, sit indoors.

1. **Begin by doing Whole Body Breathing that you learned on page 104**

   Do this until your body and mind are relaxed. Experiment with your eyes closed and opened.

2. **Get grounded by putting your awareness in your feet. If you feel ungrounded while doing this exercise, return your attention to your feet.**

   If necessary, stop the exercise by putting your hand over your solar plexus, and get up and walk around. Then shake your hands, arms, and the rest of your body. If needed, use some of the techniques to disconnect that you learned earlier, or go to Chapter 5 for additional suggestions.

3. **Extend your breath into the room you are in.**

   Just be with the room; breathe with the room. Stay away from trying to figure anything out. Just be present for a few moments. Then pull your energy and breath back into your body so that you know clearly that all of your energy and breath have returned to you, and you are free of any of the energy or breath in the place with which you just connected.

   Continue to extend your energy and breath into the following locations, remembering to completely pull your energy and breath back to your body after you extend it to each location, like:

   • The yard around your home

   • A specific tree, flower, or other part of Nature

   • The sidewalk

   • The street

   • The curb at the other side of the street

   • To anything you choose

Breathe ...

4. **Do a final disconnect from whatever you last chose to connect with.**

   Sit for a while with your eyes open and sense what's going on in your body. Are you clearly disconnected from the locations in this exercise? If not, go wash your hands, and then do something physical.

5. **You can extend your energy and breath awareness into anything to get psychic insights.**

   Practice with this exercise to strengthen your ability to extend your energy awareness to be with something.

Tools to Increase Your Nature Awareness

JUST BE IN NATURE

Sense Nature in all its settings—in the country, the mountains, the woods, the backyard, even the bit of Nature peeking out between the cracks in the cement on city streets.

- Do this daily for a couple minutes or longer periods as time allows.
- Turn off music devices, cell phones, and other noise producing equipment.
- Get your body on the ground and feel the Earth. Sometimes take your shoes off and feel the dirt, the grass, the water—Nature!

BREATHE WITH NATURE

This creates a bond between Nature and you.

- Put your hands on a tree. Perhaps lean your whole body up against the tree.
- What do you sense, including vibrations, emotions, temperature, colors, words, and images?
- Breathe with your whole body, and when you are aware of your own body, shift the breath, so that you are sensing the tree breathe.
- Do this exercise with other parts of Nature, such as the ground, grass, a bush, a leaf, flowers, and rocks. See if you can expand your breath to breathe with the whole of Nature around you. Can you feel a consciousness in Nature separate from you?

Exercise to Increase Your Nature Awareness:

READ A STONE OR CRYSTAL

Use your clairsentient and clairvoyant skills to read a stone/crystal. Get in that connected, quiet zone. Hold a stone in your non-dominant palm. Put your awareness inside the stone. Breathe with the stone, and be with it before reading it. Sense characteristics of the stone with your palm (texture, temperature, movement/vibration, emotion), and then allow clairvoyant images or other "clairs" to give you additional insights.

What was your experience?

Tools to Increase Your Nature Awareness:

TALK WITH NATURE

- At times, you might want to combine breathing and talking with Nature.

  Once a connection is made with your breath, ask the tree (or something else in Nature) a question, "How are you today?" or "What message do you have today?"

  Allow a dialogue between the tree and you to unfold.

  Try breathing and talking with Nature.

- Get in the habit of asking Nature how she is doing. For example, when you walk in the yard or anywhere, ask, "How is it going today flowers?" Allow a dialogue to unfold. It's okay if you pretend, because the psychic sense is a function of the imagination.

- When you go outside, instead of rushing to the car, take a moment to look at the sky and the surrounding Nature. Say something about what you sense, *e.g.,* "Spring is in the air today!" or say hello to Nature, a favorite tree, or plant. You may want to find one or two areas of Nature that you regularly communicate with psychically.

- Connect with something in Nature to get psychic insights. Experiment with asking questions of Nature. Some examples: your favorite tree, a creek, a bird, or a cloud. You don't need to be outside to project your awareness with Nature, so you can do this at anytime and anywhere. Make the connection with your body and breath awareness. When you feel connected to the aspect of Nature you have chosen, ask questions about anything and expect a response that will give you information. Use all your "clairs."

FIVE ANIMAL SPORTS QIGONG

- Although this could have been included in the Body Awareness section, this particular approach to Qigong uses a connection to five animals. Connecting with Nature, including animals, is a way to increase your sensitivities to energy.

- This is one of the oldest QiGong techniques, and it can improve your health as well as your psychic energy awareness.

- DVD: *Five Animal Sports QiGong,* by Dr. Yan, Jwing-Ming and Kathy K. Yang

NURTURE A PLANT

- Connect with the cycles of Nature by watching plants grow. You don't need a garden to do this. You can enjoy other people's gardens, or get a packet of seeds and start your own plant or garden inside.

- Learn how to care for a plant.

- Check on the plant each day for its needs, as well as to connect with the energy of the plant.

- Breathe with the plant every day. This will build a bond between the plant and you.

- Send it healing energy, sense energy coming from the plant, and talk to it on a daily basis.

  Put both hands one to two inches away from the plant.

  What does the plant's energy feel like?

  Send energy to the plant with your hands.

  Talk with the plant, "Would you like some energy?"

  This is effective, even if you do this for just brief periods of time.

Do you remember as a child sitting on the edge of a creek or pond and gazing into the water? As a child, I did a lot of gazing, particularly when I was in Nature. At these times, I wasn't thinking or trying or doing. I was just being in a space not in my regular world. I looked outside the window of my second-grade class, and my eyes glazed over as I merged with the oak trees. And that's why I put "scrying" under "Nature Awareness." Kids used to do a lot of nothing—just gazing. And all that spaced-out dreaminess got me into a psychic zone.

I met a psychic who was told by her mother that she used to sit at the edge of the creek and talk to something in the water. The psychic saw images and people's faces and talked with them. She now uses a scrying mirror as part of her psychic readings.

Nostradamus, sixteenth-century seer and healer, is said to have received his predictions of the future by using a bowl of water with black ink added so he couldn't see the bottom. That's a scrying tool. Black mirrors made of onyx can also be used. In my classes, I needed an easier and cheaper tool. So I bought yards of black felt that I cut in 2' x 2' squares. My students love this mind-focusing tool. Internal mind chatter is set aside, giving your psychic sense an avenue to be expressed and listened to.

1. Find a natural pond, creek, ocean, or lake.

2. Sit on the ground. Use your favorite relaxation technique. Feel the ground; perhaps breathe with the ground.

3. Stare at the water, while letting your eyes go out of focus, maybe even getting watery.

4. Begin breathing with the water (or other scrying tool you have selected).

5. Ask a question, and allow images to appear in the water. You can use any of the "clairs."

Create Your Package!

TIP FOR DISCONNECTING:	What are you thinking about yourself right now? Do you have mind chatter?
	Imagine you are standing under a shower head, or even better, under a beautiful waterfall. The water flows over your body, taking any stuff that's getting in your way deep into the healing waters below. Know that your thoughts and any mind chatter are being healed.

Answers to Your Question

READ USING CLAIRSENTIENCE AND CLAIRVOYANCE

Pair up (or do this just for yourself). Select a scrying tool to focus your mind.

Get in that connected, quiet zone. Put your awareness/energy inside the scrying tool (clairsentience). Then gaze at the tool, allowing it to take you into a relaxed state. When you are ready, your partner asks a question. Allow images to appear either in the scrying tool or in your mind (clairvoyance). When you get something, go right back into the energy of what you got, and ask for more psychic insights—not your opinion or interpretation. Give your partner everything you get psychically—no advice or interpretation of what you got—just the psychic insights.

Record insights in your journal. Interpret and analyze the psychic information. What do you think your psychic sense is trying to tell you? Using your own good judgment, what do you think is the best step for you to take now? Taking action on your psychic insights makes your psychic skills even stronger!

7 Games
HAVE FUN!

> Every August, my dad finally got time off, and we loaded up our green Chrysler station wagon and traveled to campgrounds—before that was a cool thing to do. I remember Dad taking us on hikes, picking up leaves, and telling us what tree they came from. He peeled bark off of a sassafras bush, and that's when I learned that my favorite tasty soda came from this wonderful bush. (Vacations were one of the few times we got sodas.)
>
> I have three sisters, and the four of us could be a lot to handle on family vacations. My ingenious mother came up with all kinds of car games to settle us down. One of those games was "I Spy." One sister would select an item in the car, and the rest of us asked questions about the object to figure out what she was "spying." When I look back on this now, it was a wonderful psychic game!
>
> But it wasn't fun for me when one particular sister did the selection. I just knew (a.k.a. psychically knew) that when I got close, she changed what she had selected. I could feel it. Of course, that just ended in our fighting over this.
>
> Mom's efforts, unfortunately, didn't always work.

It's not important whether you win or play the following games "right." It's important that you exercise your psychic muscle. Relax and have fun. If you are wrong, chuckle lightly, instead of becoming critical of yourself. This helps shift any self-criticism and performance anxiety laid down in the neural pathways in your brain.

Anticipation Games

These games are fun little exercises to play with your psychic sense. Before you are about to do something, anticipate what will happen by asking yourself: How many? What's about to happen? Who will be there?

Play the anticipation games by yourself, with children, or other adults. You can play this game using anything. Here are some ideas to get you started:

Who's on the phone?
Without looking at the caller ID, use your psychic sense to determine who is calling (or who is at the door).

Where's the parking space?
When looking for a parking space, ask your psychic sense where to turn to find the best space for you. I bet you already do this.

How many new emails or text messages are in my in-box?
As you bring up your email or text messages, guess how many new messages are in your in-box.

At what store will I find what I'm looking for?
Before shopping, pause and relax; then ask your psychic sense what store will have what you want at the best price. Let the insight come to you instead of figuring this out based on your knowledge of the stores. This is also a helpful way to find a great restaurant or a gift for someone!

WHAT'S IN THE BOX?

Get a plain box. Put an object in the box. The object will be easier to read if it is simple. The players put their hands around the box (without moving it) and make notes about what they are getting. When every person is finished reading, the group shares their notes and discusses the experience. This is a great game at your next party or barbeque! And the winner gets the prize inside the box.

I SPY

One person decides what object they will focus on in the room. The person then mentally sends the image to those playing the game. The receivers ask questions they get psychically about the object. This is a fun game to play in the car (not the driver) especially if you want to get children to quiet down and focus their energy (as on my childhood camping trips!)

TELEPATHIC MESSAGE

Get a friend to join you in this game. Decide who will be the sender and who will be the receiver. The sender "sends" a telepathic message of a specific word, thought, or image to the receiver frequently during the day. The receiver periodically relaxes and expects to receive the message. It doesn't matter whether the sender and receiver do this at the same time. Later in the day, the two of you compare notes.

PERSON IN THE MIDDLE

This game works best if everyone knows each other. If they aren't familiar, it can easily be played with both men and women—this time identifying the gender of the person around the person in the middle. Four other people quietly move into position—one in front, one in back, and one to either side of the blindfolded person in the middle—about two feet away. One of the four people rings a bell indicating they are ready for the reading to begin.

The person in the middle gets into that connected, quiet zone. Put your energy in front of you. Using your "clairs," who is the person or what gender is the person? Continue to shift your awareness around you until all the people are read.

PSYCHIC ANTIQUING

Go to an antique store. Hold objects, and use the instructions for psychometry on page 108 to read the personality of the previous owner. You will never know if you are correct. But that's not the point. For now, you will be getting valuable experience exercising your psychic sense.

HIDE AND SEEK

Recall Helen Gilman who read tea leaves in Boulder, Colorado, in the early twentieth century. When she was a child, her mother hid candy in the house for Helen and her sister to find. The first to find the candy got it. Psychic Helen was almost always the first. A great psychic game, even if candy as a motivator may not be so healthy!

Add a psychic dimension to this popular children's game. This approach can be used to find lost items, too.

- One person hides and stays in the same place until the game is over. The others find the hidden person by pooling their psychic senses into a circle.
- The seekers get in a circle, hold hands, and fill the circle with energy. Pretend the circle is filled with beautiful light.
- The seekers picture the hidden person standing inside the circle. Think about the hidden person—personality, clothes, hair color. (If you are using this to find a lost or hidden object, feel your connection to it, see the color, and imagine yourself using the object.)
- Each person states aloud what they psychically sense about the room the person has hidden in. Include furniture, objects, colors, smells, sounds, and feelings. This should narrow the possible location of the hidden person.

- The seekers go to the room based on their psychic insights. If the person isn't in the room, just laugh, and remember that you will get better at this. Then the seekers run around looking for the hidden person. Repeat the game; you will gain skills.

PSYCHIC GO FISH
See instructions on page 107.

Create Your Package!

TIP FOR DISCONNECTING:	When doing the "Reading Envelope Options" exercise that follows, do one of the following for about three minutes after reading each envelope:

- Wash your hands
- Go outside and sit on the ground
- Do something physical

Then come back to the exercise and read the next envelope until all three envelopes are read.

Answers to Your Question

READING ENVELOPE OPTIONS

Now that you have used several approaches to getting insights to answer your question, use this technique to consider potential actions you might take. Evaluate the psychic insights using your analytical, thinking mind. Based on your assessment, make a list of possible options or next steps you might take concerning your question.

Write each option on a piece of paper, and put each one in an envelope. It's helpful to have three to five options—enough to have choice, but not so many that it's overwhelming. Mix up the envelopes so you don't know which option is in a particular envelope.

Pick one envelope, and use one of the many techniques you have learned in the workbook to do a psychic reading on that option. See the list of reading techniques in Chapter 6, page 189. To get additional insights, ask a friend or a professional psychic to give you a psychic reading on the envelopes without opening them.

When all readings are complete, open the envelopes and compare the readings to select the best next steps for you to take.

NOTES

CHAPTER 5

Getting Unstuck
Create the "Package" for Your Psychic Abilities

Brian regularly senses lots of spirits around him. He tried getting help from a famous psychic and has tried innumerous ways to get them to go away. The spirits leave for a while, but then inevitably return. They won't leave him alone, and he wants it to stop.

Cassie is constantly overwhelmed by psychic insights coming to her on a daily basis. She tries using the many tools and techniques she learns from our faculty. Still, a year later, she is overwhelmed and has little or no control over her abilities. Cassie is one of the more gifted students, but she doesn't have effective use of her abilities.

Gabriela gives psychic insights to people all the time. She regularly gets psychic information when talking with her friends, and she lets them know that. A few years later, after Gabriela had gotten married and then divorced, some members of the group commented that they knew this would happen. A new member of the group asked if they had shared their thoughts with their friend. "Oh no, Gabriela is the psychic!"

Donna often walks into a room of people and feels drained when she leaves. She has always taken on the mannerisms and emotions of others. Now that Donna is taking psychic classes, she finds that her body mirrors the health problems of the people she reads.

It doesn't matter how psychic you are, if you can't effectively use your abilities. And that requires creating a strong foundation that includes good ethics and boundaries, tools for grounding and disconnecting from psychic energy, and the ability to get unstuck. It's what I call "the package," and it provides a framework, a container for your psychic abilities to thrive. The first step in creating that package is to take responsibility for your psychic development.

Ultimately, psychic development is an individual, internal process. No one can make you psychic. There is no secret code or magic spell that can make you psychic. It requires you to be in a zone, like in meditation, and you must get yourself there—no one can do that for you. Because being psychic requires you to allow insights to come to you, you have to be able to take yourself to that quiet place inside of you and let that happen—no one can do that for you.

In Chapter 2, I gave you three "Gs" to use when you get struck or frustrated when using your psychic abilities. Now it's time for the fourth "G": **Get over yourself!** You are responsible for getting out of your own way and not allowing emotional interferences or other blocks to stop you from accessing your psychic abilities. Don't wallow in self-pity or whine about not being able to access your abilities (okay, a little bit is normal—a lot, is a problem). Don't allow yourself to feel overwhelmed by energy, spirits, or anything psychic—this is often about your own underlying psychological/emotional matters, not your psychic ability itself. And you need to deal with this to be more psychic.

Ultimately, you have to let yourself be psychic. For example, in the beginning of psychic development, students are often annoyed by the clock ticking or noises outside the classroom. That's understandable. But you can teach yourself to get in the quiet zone where you can access your psychic sense in spite of noise. The only reason you may not know how to do this now is because you probably weren't taught how to get into a psychic space. Or you were psychic as a kid, but it was "taught" out of you. Psychic ability is a learned skill, so with this workbook and practice, you can develop this skill just like any other skill and use it when you choose to!

You are ultimately responsible for moving past your own self-esteem issues that contribute to self-doubt and frustration, as well as other possible internal unconscious blocks. It is up to you to know when to seek counsel in the form of therapy to move through any emotional issues that may arise as you attempt to further develop psychic ability. This is about your willingness to embrace the ongoing development of your inner self by working with your body, mind, and spirit. In my experience, when people open their psychic abilities, whatever is going on in their unconscious mind that needs attention will present itself. And that needs to be addressed if you want to have full access to your psychic abilities.

I always had experienced psychic abilities in my life. But as I mentioned earlier, it was massage school that pried the door open even further. Along with it, I was challenged to deal with the trauma of child sexual abuse that still resided in my body and in the unhealed recesses of my mind. I had been in psychotherapy in the past. But as my body awareness increased in massage school, and as I received somatic Cranio-Sacral Therapy, it was like the metal top had popped off a pressure cooker, and steam was going everywhere.

I experienced psychic knowings without asking for them. I felt even more deeply the burdens and difficulties that people were grappling with. Without asking for it, I vividly relived childhood events that I thought I had already dealt with in therapy. This reliving included both positive and negative experiences. It was as though my psychic ability and childhood memories were bouncing off the walls, and I had no control over either of them.

Every week for two months, my cranio-sacral therapist encouraged me to see a psychotherapist due to the abuse issues coming up in our work. I had been to therapists. I don't know why I was so reluctant to see another one, but finally I did see one, and that's when I got back my psychic abilities more fully. I healed some deeper issues about my childhood that, looking back, I seemed to have only skimmed the surface of in prior therapy. I had been sexually assaulted by a deacon and pillar of my childhood church. Up to that point, it had been easier to stuff that away, but I had lost a lot of things in my life—joy, a healthy life partnership, and a fuller expression of my psychic sense.

Not everyone has this level of stuff stored away in their unconscious minds. But you likely have something there—we all do because nearly everyone has experienced some life problems. I remember this happening during dream groups I led. When new group members started working with their dreams, they were often surprised that something from their pasts came up with the first series of dreams. I've seen it with students in psychic classes as well. When we take the time to pause and listen to a deeper part of ourselves, problematic experiences often resurface.

We spend much of our day not listening to our inner self. So when we turn to listen by meditating, doing hypnosis, taking psychic development classes, or focusing on our dreams, this part of us is eager to communicate what it likely has been trying to tell us for a long time. But we haven't been paying attention.

I tell students that it's the unconscious mind saying "Hello" to us—glad that we've come for a visit. Addressing what this part of us has to say won't take years of therapy, and you don't have to wait to be psychic until you deal with what lies in the inner recesses of your mind. You just need a willingness to embrace the whole of your being. And that means listening to the sometimes uneasy leftovers from living life.

I learned in hypnosis school that when the conscious mind wants to do something—like be psychic, and the unconscious mind has leftover stuff from the past that disagrees with or gets in the way of that conscious desire, the unconscious mind wins. You can't bypass your stuff to be psychic. It will likely come say "Hello" to you, and I'm guessing that it has already done that this far into the workbook.

The first step in dealing with unconscious mind stuff is to understand how awareness functions in relation to the psychic sense. Study the chart that follows, and begin asking what might be lodged in your unconscious mind that's not just getting in the way of your psychic abilities, but also your life in general. I'll give you ways to move through sociological, psychological, and physical blocks.

We need effective use of all aspects of the mind.
A healthy unconscious mind allows for greater access to psychic awareness.

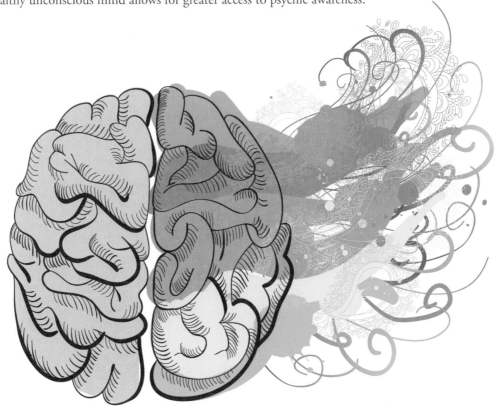

EXPANDED AWARENESS

- Expanded awareness
- Psychic sense
- Oneness; interconnection
- Imagination; creativity

UNCONSCIOUS MIND

- Beliefs
- Stored memory
- Effects of trauma
- What gets triggered
- Unhealthy ego needs from unresolved stuff
- When there is conflict between what you want for your life and what the unconscious mind believes, the unconscious mind wins.

CONSCIOUS MIND

- Thinks
- Analyzes
- Interprets
- *Looks* for insights
- Decides
- Gets in the way of psychic knowing but is needed to evaluate psychic insights

1 Blocks to Your Psychic Abilities

(AND WHAT TO DO ABOUT THEM)

Three months into her training at the Aspen Program, Bobbie came to me concerned that her psychic abilities had shut down. She told me that she had always been psychic, but since taking classes, she was stuck. Bobbie wasn't getting much psychic information during class exercises, and when she did, it was wrong.

Devon never considered herself psychic. But at the first class, she clearly "saw" what was in the bag when I placed it on her table. Other students in class were impressed and congratulated her. Devon never got anything correct after that. She is not alone. Students are surprised at how good they are at the psychic exercises in class, only to experience it shut down for weeks and sometimes months.

Jodie wants to be psychic, but she is pretty negative about herself, so she doesn't think she can develop these abilities. Over a six-month period of taking classes, Jodie barely makes progress. Her classmates are aware she has a negative outlook on life, but they stick with her, helping her to improve her abilities. Just when she finally makes a breakthrough, she quits the program.

We all have blocks to our psychic sense, even professional psychics—because we are human. In my experience, blocks come in three ways: sociological (the world out there), psychological (the world inside you), and physical (your body, energy, and health). You might want to come back to this chapter over time to explore the ideas offered here to move through these blocks. It's not something you can do just while going through this workbook. Come back to the material to continue your evolution—it's about living life fully, not just increasing your psychic abilities.

Techniques are growing in popularity to quickly clear problems, negative thinking, and past trauma. They include creating your own reality, intending, eye movement, and tapping the body. While these may be helpful to move through blocks, there is something even more important than just getting past old stuff. And that is the self-awareness that we gain as we move through the process of dealing with the emotional fallout from negative experiences. Some of these techniques are used to bypass the process of self-introspection and self-understanding. Self-knowledge is what you gain when you actually grapple with what's going on in your life before using techniques to clear them. Keep this in mind as you work with blocks to your psychic abilities.

If you have been doing the lessons in this workbook and find that you still experience blocks, then it's time to focus on something deeper going on in your life. If the mind chatter persists, it may be time to explore what may be blocking your access to your psychic sense. There could be any number of things contributing to the mind chatter block. Or perhaps you are procrastinating, not using the material here even though you want to have stronger abilities. Blocks can come in many forms. The following can get you started in figuring out what type of block you are experiencing:

I made a decision to tell the truth about what I really do for a living when the next person asked me. And the first person I told was Jesus. Yep, and I'll get to that.

It was the first year of the Aspen Program, and I figured it was hypocritical for me to teach people to value their psychic abilities when I was in the closet about mine. So, I picked up the phone and called my parents, who lived in another state, to tell them what I really did for a living. Up until then, I'd told everyone I was a hypnotherapist. This was kind of true, but by the end of the first year of the Aspen Program, my psychic work took over, and I hardly did any individual hypnotherapy sessions.

I was concerned that my psychotherapist father would pull something out of the DSM (Diagnostic and Statistical Manual of Mental Disorders) used to label people with mental health problems. I was surprised when Dad said, "Well, I have had those experiences as well." We went on to discuss the ways in which both of us used this basic human function. What a relief! Even at my age, the fear of criticism and judgment about being psychic still controlled me.

One afternoon, I handed several checks to the bank teller to be deposited to my business account. He was just being polite, doing small talk, when he asked me what kind of business I did. I had made the personal commitment that the very next person who asked, I would be honest about what I did for a living. And it was Jesus. That was the name on his badge. Now, I know that it's pronounced "Hay-Seuss." Still, I like telling that story. Frankly, I don't think Jesus Christ would mind. But that's a story for a different book.

I regularly meet people who suffer from being psychic. Some had psychic experiences as kids and shut it down because their family either didn't encourage it or just told them not to talk about it again. It's not comforting to know that these same family members often have above-average psychic abilities themselves.

We live in a society that doesn't value things psychic and often makes fun of it. This compounds the problem of developing and accessing our abilities. Below are suggestions to help you disarm some of the social impact of being psychic.

Just a matter of learning. We don't teach our children in school how to develop their innate psychic sense. Although successful scientists, artists, and business professionals claim to use intuition, we don't teach students in colleges and universities that these people did this, much less how the students can develop their own abilities. So part of the sociological block has to do with your not being given the opportunity to learn how to be psychic. As you do the exercises in this workbook and get practice, your abilities will grow. Some blocks are just learning blocks that time and practice will clear!

Write a "Psychic Life Review." Identify messages from adults, friends, teachers, and society that have been sent to you about things psychic. Review your life from the youngest age to now, and write in your journal about the times when you got negative and positive messages about your psychic abilities. Also include messages you received about psychic matters in general. Examples: A show on television about ghosts was ridiculed by your parents. As a child (or even as a grown-up), you overheard adults talking negatively about psychics. If you had an imaginary friend or saw/felt spirits as a child, how did your parents handle this? What do your friends and family think about your desire to develop your psychic abilities? Students who have taken the time to do a psychic life review have come up with a considerable amount of memories that helped them move through sociological blocks.

Get support. Join or create a small support group of individuals interested in developing and using their psychic abilities. It's helpful to have such a group to counteract the sometimes negative feedback about things psychic. The group can also provide support for processing insights you gained from your psychic life review. A support system is part of creating the "package" for your psychic abilities.

Educate yourself about things psychic in our society. Do an Internet search of prominent mainstream people who have used psychic insights, like Bill Gates, Steve Jobs, Colin Powell, Jonas Salk, Abraham Lincoln, and Albert Einstein. Often belittled as "women's intuition," women have also claimed to use the psychic sense as well—my favorites: Harriet Tubman and Barbara McClintock (cell geneticist, Nobel laureate, and mother of epigenetics). Check out my list on www.PsychicIQ.com. Discovering that individuals have always valued things psychic helps undermine sociological blocks to the psychic sense.

What Are Your Blocks?

A HALLWAY OF DOORS

Use this technique to discover blocks you might not already know about, or to get added insights into the blocks that you are aware of.

Get in a relaxed space, with both your body and mind grounded and centered.

Imagine you are walking down a hallway with many doors on either side of you. As you walk, set the clear intention that you will be drawn to the very door that you need to go to, so that you will get additional insights about blocks to your psychic abilities.

Allow yourself to be drawn to a specific door. When you get there, stand in front of it for a few moments. What does the door look like? Feel like?

Reach for the doorknob. Open the door. If you need assistance, ask a spirit guide or loved one in spirit to accompany you. Know that when you walk inside, you will immediately have a specific experience that gives you insights into your blocks.

Psychological Blocks

I was stuck, and I knew it. In the early days of being a psychic, my clients gave positive feedback to me. But I knew something was missing. I had been getting readings since the 1970s, and most of those readings had more precognitive advice than I was giving to my clients. I suspected it had something to do with my childhood.

So, I used hypnotherapy to age regress to whatever experience I had in childhood that had something to do with a possible block to knowing the future. I'm not suggesting that the future is set in stone. But it can be helpful if I can give psychic advice on where my client's life is trending.

During hypnosis, an experience from childhood presented itself. I see myself stringing beans with a teenager on the steps of a house out in the country. When I was a child, my family regularly took day trips in the summer to visit family, old friends, and historical sites.

I remember the scene. We were visiting people my parents knew in a rural town in Virginia. I felt lucky the teenager in the family chose me to string beans with her. So we sat on the front porch talking and enjoying the summer evening.

Then a young man came down the sidewalk, and my newfound friend was excited to see him. It was her boyfriend. I always had this memory. But now, regressed to that experience again, I realized more had been going on than I had originally recalled.

As I had sat there stringing beans, spikes of electricity darted from him into my stomach. Adrenaline rushed up my back and filled my throat so I couldn't talk. They should have seen that I was beet-red, but they were so excited to see each other that I was invisible to them. I knew deep in my being that this guy was going to physically harm this young woman. I didn't know when or how. Left unexpressed, because I knew by then not to say things that didn't make sense to people, my anxiety roared to the point that I was sure he was going to kill her.

I have no idea what happened to her or if she was ever hurt by him. But I was left with a psychic trauma stored in my unconscious mind that resurfaced whenever I psychically got that something physical might happen to someone I cared about. Several times, I was sure my father or mother was going to die, only to find out that it was a lesser health problem. Before remembering what I had psychically experienced the day I was stringing beans, I always overreacted to my precognitions about friends and family members' health issues. After doing some healing on this, I got more precognitions about my clients as well as for myself.

We all have stuff—leftover trauma, beliefs, and memories stored in our unconscious minds. This unresolved stuff doesn't have to be about something psychic, like in my experience stringing beans. It can be about anything, like not growing up in a loving, caring home or no one being there for you when you skinned your knee after falling from your bicycle. Dealing with your inner, psychological stuff is like peeling an onion—it's an on-going, healing spiral. You deal with an issue and move on with life, only to find that down the road another layer of the onion is calling to be healed. Your willingness to embrace these learning opportunities is what living a conscious, intentional life is all about.

Model for Understanding How Trauma Affects Us

THE HEALTHIER AND CLEARER YOUR UNCONSCIOUS MIND, THE GREATER ACCESS YOU HAVE TO YOUR PSYCHIC SENSE

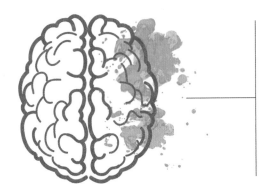

Trauma is stored in the right brain. Some view imagination, creativity, and intuition as a right-brain activity.

When you seek to develop your psychic abilities, increase your body awareness though hands-on work, or use other mind-quieting techniques, the trauma may shift or release to some degree.

Then, your "stuff" becomes more apparent and accessible. Perhaps even stuff you have already dealt with. We all have stuff—it's the human condition.

Fear of spirits and anxiety about thinking that when you open your psychic abilities you won't be able to close or control them often originate with other fears that have nothing to do with things psychic.

If you have excessive fear, do some inner work to discover why this is happening and what caused it.

Regardless of where it came from, the solution is within you.

What is Psychological Health?

WHAT IT *DOESN'T* MEAN:

1. That you are happy, successful, and healthy; and you are with your soul mate and have wonderful friends...a.k.a., everything in your life is wonderful!

2. That once you do your inner, psychological work, you've done it; you're healed; you won't need to do any more.

3. That once you do your inner, psychological work, or you are doing your soul's purpose or setting your intentions, that you will no longer attract negative or difficult life experiences. Positive thinking, intending, and creating your own reality can be empowering tools. But they are not replacements for doing your inner work—the stuff in your unconscious mind.

WHAT IT *DOES* MEAN:

1. You are able to identify when something is affecting you, *i.e.*, creating stress, trauma, confusion, pain, depression, etc.

2. You have a pretty good idea where #1 is coming from within you—what it is triggering in you.

3. You have resources that assist you to move through it (#1).

HOW TO *GET* IT: (PSYCHOLOGICAL HEALTH IS A PROCESS NOT A DESTINATION)

1. Know your family system and your role in it. Understanding your family issues will help you heal, even if your family members will not or cannot join you in the healing process.

2. Know your psychological, emotional makeup.

3. Create good boundaries.

4. Get in touch with your body awareness.

5. Learn how to quiet your mind.

6. Get physically healthy.

7. Include creativity and on-going learning in your life.

8. Create healthy relationships: friends, family, small group support, and colleagues.

9. Explore what lies beyond the personal (the transpersonal, spirituality, science).

10. Healthy people are introspective and reflective.

What is a Trigger?

IF YOU'RE HUMAN, YOU EXPERIENCE THEM.

A trigger is a reminder about something that happened in the past that is causing anxiety and/or similar emotions in the now—whether or not you are aware of it. Too often, we aren't aware that something in our psychological makeup (unconscious mind) is being triggered. When we get triggered, we react in ways that aren't totally about what is happening in the moment. When we get triggered, we react, in part, because of something in the past that created stress or anxiety.

When you are consciously aware of when and why you are being triggered, you have more choice, so, you don't react out of an unconscious need to repair or act out something that happened to you in the past.

Sure, your reaction to the current life experiences can be totally appropriate. But to the extent that you are responding from a place of unresolved issues from your past, stored in your unconscious mind, then you aren't running your life, your unconscious mind is.

You aren't in charge.

Think how you might respond differently if you clean out old stuff from your unconscious mind.

How might your life be different?

How might your psychic abilities be different?

MOST OF US DON'T KNOW WHEN WE ARE BEING TRIGGERED.

Here are some signs:
1. Overreaction to what is happening

2. Repeating the same problematic pattern of experience over and over

3. Depression; feeling numb to life

4. Feelings of being overwhelmed

5. Thinking you don't have any problems and everything in your childhood was wonderful! (a.k.a., denial)

6. Avoiding the problem

7. Not looking within

8. Intense emotions of any type that are disabling

Following are questions to use to explore your psychological health. I totally get it that some people think that if they focus on the past, they won't be able to create the future they want. Doing your inner, psychological work is important because the unconscious mind, where all that stuff lies, controls any conscious efforts you might make to create your own reality. So use tools to do healing work with that part of you. Still more important, self-awareness about your childhood and your life in general makes you a well-rounded person. Complete the review below and revisit it a year from now.

Date: ....

Psychological Health Review

In what ways have you worked on your childhood issues? What have you learned about yourself having done this?

_____
_____
_____
_____
_____
_____
_____
_____
_____
_____
_____
_____
_____
_____
_____
_____

Do you know what your unfinished childhood issues are? Describe.

_____
_____
_____
_____
_____
_____
_____
_____
_____
_____
_____
_____
_____
_____
_____
_____
_____
_____

What tools do you currently use to maintain good psychological health? (*e.g.*, journaling, meditation, dreamwork, self-reflection)

What outside resources do you have for maintaining your psychological health? State name and type. (*e.g.*, therapists, bodyworkers, support groups)

What outside resources do you have for maintaining your psychological health? State name and type. (*e.g.*, therapists, bodyworkers, support groups)

_____
_____
_____
_____
_____
_____
_____
_____
_____
_____
_____
_____
_____
_____
_____
_____
_____
_____
_____
_____
_____

My personal strengths: (Revisit this from Chapter Two) Imagine you are at a job interview and the prospective employer asks you what you bring to the job, but in this case, it's what you bring to life in general.

_____
_____
_____
_____
_____
_____
_____
_____
_____
_____
_____
_____
_____
_____
_____
_____
_____
_____
_____

The most significant life problem, block, or other life issue I am experiencing now and how I am addressing it: This is NOT about your psychic abilities—it's about your life. (Revisit this from Chapter Two.)

What Are Your Blocks?

THE WATERFALL:

Use this technique to discover blocks you might not already know about or to get added insights into the blocks that you are already aware of.

Get in a relaxed space, with both your body and mind grounded and centered.

Imagine you are standing near the top of a waterfall. Reach inside your body and pull out energy that no longer serves you, and drop it at the top of the waterfall. See it go into the pool of healing waters at the bottom of the falls, knowing this stuff of yours will be healed by the waters. Include childhood issues, problems you are having now in your life, and blocks to your life and psychic abilities that you already know about. Continue clearing out all the clutter until you think you are done.

Then one last time, reach deep inside your body and pull out whatever else is getting in your way—stuff you are not aware of. Hold the energy of it in your hands. Look at it. Do you know what it is? Then drop it into the waterfall, letting it go now so you can be more psychic and so you can enjoy your life!

Physical Blocks

A woman came up to me after a talk I gave about the Aspen Program for Psychic Development. She said, "I realize that I came here for one thing. When you said that some people drink to close down their psychic abilities, I understood that. You've helped me so much just with that one thing. Thank you." Some people drink to shut down the overwhelming sense that spirits are around them and won't leave them alone. I eat to close down my abilities. I prefer brownies over alcohol. Of course, these efforts may only temporarily close down psychic abilities. And the back door to your unconscious is left open and unattended, particularly with drinking.

Madison can't feel her body, and she doesn't understand my exercises for putting energy awareness into a question or with a person she is reading. I ask her to pretend, but she just doesn't get what I'm saying. Madison always thought she could feel her own body, but she has no sense of the energy moving in and around her.

Nan has always had above-average psychic abilities. After menopause, it just didn't come as easily as it once did. She used to be pretty on target with her psychic advice. But now even she senses her psychic guidance has been watered down. Nan wonders if it has something to do with her hormonal or other body changes.

Body awareness is psychic awareness. If you can't feel your body, this may be a helpful starting point for moving through blocks of any type. Fortunately, today there are many techniques and practitioners to assist you in becoming more body aware, including Reiki, chakra balancing, and any type of energywork. The overall health of your body contributes to your being able to better access your psychic abilities. Chapter 4 provided techniques for increasing body awareness.

Be well. The health of your physical body is vital to effectively accessing your psychic sense. Seek out a trained nutritionist, naturopathic physician, acupuncturist, or other holistic health practitioner to create health and wellness in your body. Learn what foods, vitamins, and supplements hinder (as well as support) your health. Below are some resources on health and wellness. I am not a licensed health practitioner, so what follows are for you to check out with the appropriate professional.

American College for the Advancement of Medicine

www.acamnet.org

Carotec

Supplements and alternative health information with critiques of Western medicine.
www.carotec.com

Dr. Mercola

Osteopathic physician
His email list provides up-to-date information on alternative health information with critiques of Western medicine.
www.Mercola.com

Dr. Oz

www.doctoroz.com

Institute of Functional Medicine

www.functionalmedicine.org

Life Enhancement

Supplements; alternative health information with critiques of Western medicine.
http://life-enhancement.com

Life Extension Foundation

Alternative health protocols for most diseases based on research.
www.lef.org

Mary Enig

Researched trans-fats since the 1960s. Check out her book: *Know Your Fats: The Complete Primer for Understanding the Nutrition of Fats, Oils and Cholesterol,* Bethesda Press, 2000.

Natural Standard

Research on alternative medicine.
www.Naturalstandard.com

Organic Consumers Association

Stay in touch with the latest on food and more. Stay connected politically to what is happening to our food and supplements. You can get on their email list.
www.organicconsumers.org

Price-Pottenger Nutritional Foundation

Based on the work of Weston A. Price and Frances M. Pottenger on optimal health through diet.
www.ppnf.org

Sally Fallon

Incorporated Mary Enig's principles and others in her book, *Nourishing Traditions: The Cookbook that Challenges Politically Correct Nutrition and the Diet Dictocrats,* Newtrends Publishing, Inc.; Revised and Updated 2nd edition (April 8, 2003).

Weston A. Price Foundation

Weston Price researched "isolated nonindustrial peoples" to determine optimal health and diet.
www.westonaprice.org/

Support of the Pineal & Pituitary Glands. The pineal and pituitary glands are part of your psychic sense. So the health of these glands (as well as your overall endocrine system) may be important to effectively access and use psychic abilities. Below are websites to check out. (If the any of the web addresses are outdated, do an Internet search using most of the words in the links to find the website.) I am not a health practitioner, so you need to check this out with an appropriate professional.

1. Fluoride adversely affects the pineal gland:

- The pineal gland can become calcified because of fluoride. http://articles.mercola.com/sites/articles/archive/2011/08/09/fluoride-and-pineal-gland.aspx?SetFocus=commentfocus#commentfocus

- To detox: www.naturalnews.com/026605_fluoride_fluorides_detox.html

2. Websites with information on pineal health:

- http://dherbs.com/news/4530/4669/Pineal-Gland-Mystique/d,ai.html

- http://thewatchers.adorraeli.com/2012/01/24/why-pineal-gland-and-mental-health-are-most-important-in-these-times/

- www.fluoridealert.org/issues/health/pineal-gland/

- Pineal toning: http://ezinearticles.com/?What-is-Pineal-Toning-and-How-Do-I-Do-It?&id=2295914

- http://foodforconsciousness.blogspot.com/p/reactivating-pineal-gland.html

- www.selfgrowth.com/articles/foods_that_feed_the_pineal_gland

3. Support for the pineal gland:

- Melatonin

- Sleep in the dark with absolutely no lights on, including those on alarm clocks, televisions, plugs, etc. Light sources affect your circadian rhythm and, therefore, your pineal gland. Light that hits any part of your skin will activate the pineal gland during sleep and may interrupt sleeping.

4. Websites with information on pituitary health:

- www.marysherbs.com/anatomy/anat-pit.shtml

- www.livestrong.com/article/487203-foods-for-a-good-pituitary-gland/

- www.livestrong.com/article/149355-ayurvedic-herbs-for-the-pituitary-gland/

5. Supplements for the pituitary gland:

- Vitamins: iodine, copper, iron, magnesium: www.livestrong.com/article/348061-vitamins-minerals-for-the-pituitary-gland/

- www.seacoast.com/topic.php?health=supplements+that+support+the+pituitary+gland

What Are Your Blocks?

FLYING BLOCKS

Use this technique to discover blocks you might not already know about or to get added insights into the blocks that you are aware of.

Lie down and get comfortable. You might want a blanket to keep warm, and put a pillow under your head and knees. Close your eyes, and do whole-body breathing.

Ask your blocks to leave your body. Visualize cubes/blocks with wings flying out of your body, easily and gratefully. Feel lighter with each flying block. Now ask for a block that you aren't fully aware of to come out of your energy body and float above you.

See it fly up and out of your body. Ask, "Why are you there?" and continue having a conversation with the floating block so you better understand what's going on with blocks you might be experiencing.

When your conversation is complete, send it on its way, thanking it for giving you insights about your psychic abilities and your life.

Resources for Healing Blocks—Sociological, Psychological, and Physical

Talk therapy is important for understanding your life, but it may not be enough to remove blocks. Working with the unconscious aspects of trauma or any emotional issue is vital to removing blocks to the psychic sense. Put together a variety of resources to help you. Find the ones that suit you the best. In my experience, psychic development goes along with inner development.

Following are tools to use on your own. But also include professionals so you have "people" to go to when you can't move through stuff by yourself. Having resources to deal with blocks when they arise (and they will arise as long as you are human ☺) is part of developing a strong foundation and support system to grow your psychic abilities.

TOOLS TO HELP YOU
IDENTIFY AND MOVE THROUGH BLOCKS

- Talk Therapy
- Art Therapy
- Journaling
- Visual/Art Journaling
- Meditation (group and individual)
- Contemplation
- Hypnosis
- Self-reflection; journaling
- Art, music, creative expression
- Dreamwork
- Support groups
- Get physically healthy

- Holistic health practitioners
- Energy movement, *e.g.,* QiGong, Tai Chi, Yoga
- Any physical activity, *e.g,* walking
- Breath/Pranayama
- Body awareness exercises
- Body-centered psychotherapy
- Receive bodywork/energywork
- Reiki hands-on energy for yourself (the attunements can clear blocks in your chakras)
- Learn to communicate effectively—build healthy relationships; there are classes & books on this

2 Tools and Tips for Grounding, Centering, and Disconnecting

Some of the material in this section has already been scattered throughout this workbook to get you started on "Creating Your Package." Being able to ground, center, and disconnect are integral to psychic work. This allows you to maintain good boundaries, so you don't feel physically drained or emotionally overwhelmed. You can't do psychic work without being able to get in the space where psychic insights flow to you. Grounding and centering are what help you get in that space so you can connect to what you want to psychically read. As you develop these skills, you will be better able to gain full and effective use of your psychic abilities.

If you want to easily ground, center, and disconnect at will, make this a part of your everyday life—not just when doing psychic work. At some point, you probably won't need to use tools and techniques. They will be so deeply ingrained in your being that the abilities that come from using these techniques and tools will be there when you need them. Tools are just tools: the tools aren't making it happen—they are assisting you until you no longer need that assistance.

Let your inner guidance teach you the best ways for you to ground, center, and disconnect. As you go through this section, keep these questions in mind. You need to have ready answers to them to effectively use your psychic abilities:

1. When you are scattered, how do you ground yourself?

2. How do you quiet your mind?

3. When you feel like you've picked up someone else's stuff, how do you disconnect from it and let it go?

THE DIFFERENCE BETWEEN GROUNDED AND CENTERED

Grounded: The ability to function in the normal waking reality while using psychic abilities. Being tethered or anchored to the Earth, while accessing the psychic sense. Clients may think that, when I'm giving readings, I'm in a normal space, talking with them the way I am at other times. I'm not. I am here in this reality, while connecting to a psychic space. But it may take me a while to disconnect, so that I can drive a car.

Centered: Getting into that quiet space inside of you. Connecting with the "sweet spot" within.

Ground Yourself

Being "grounded" is being connected both to the Earth and yourself (your body, mind, and personality). It is being tethered to your Earth reality while you access your psychic sense—so you can more effectively integrate what you get psychically into our concrete realm of existence—so you don't "lose it" and become spacey.

GENERAL SUGGESTIONS:

- Breathe with your feet and the Earth.
- Send a cord from your sacrum deep into the center of the Earth.
- Surround your body with a bubble of light—use whatever color you prefer.
- Imagine you are a huge, ancient tree, and you can feel your roots going deep into the ground.
- Say a brief prayer or affirmation. You might want to say the same thing each time, so that the words quickly ground you whenever you'd like.

- Know how to connect with your own body. Ways to get in tune with your body: bodywork and energywork, body awareness exercises, energy movement, such as Qi Gong and Tai Chi, breathing exercises/pranayama. When you know your body's energy, you will be better able to sense when you are picking up energy that's not yours and release it.

- Before starting a body health reading and particularly a hands-on energy session, sense the energy in your body and know where your energy begins and ends. Maintain this awareness throughout the session. It may take effort at first, but later this will become a habit—a good habit to have!

- Use woodsy essential oils or incense (*e.g.*, pine, cedar, juniper, sandalwood, fir); stones/crystals (*e.g.*, smoky quartz, carnelian, garnet, bloodstone, black tourmaline); flower essences; or other tools you know about that are grounding.

SPECIFIC SUGGESTIONS FOR SPIRIT MEDIUMS

- Establish a gatekeeper or group of spirit guides who work with you, so that when you are doing spirit communication work, you know they will be there supporting you. This is a relationship you build over time, so that you feel secure in their support of you. Their energy can have a grounding influence for you. Before starting a reading, make a connection with them: call their names, sense them behind you, or see them in a circle around the room protecting you and the energy in the room. You might ask your spirit guides what technique they suggest you use to ground and protect the energy during spirit communication.

- Consider inviting a supportive friend or other spirit medium to join you while you read to act as a ground and perhaps a facilitator.

- Use a special crystal or stone on a regular basis just for your spirit communication work. Charge it by using some of the techniques available on the Internet (search: "how to charge crystals"). If you are working with a specific spirit guide or group, be sure to ask them to imbue/charge the stone with their energy and their connection with you.

- Wood can be very grounding. If you don't have wood floors or other wood in your psychic reading environment, use a wooden bowl. The wooden bowl can help hold/ground the energy in a room.

Center Yourself

Being "centered" is being aware and focused, as in "Be still, and know." When you are centered, you can then expand your awareness to do psychic work. The ability to be centered requires a quiet mind and body. To be centered, you must be grounded first.

GENERAL SUGGESTIONS:

- Meditation techniques
- Listening to relaxing music or playing an instrument
- Self-hypnosis
- Mindfulness (being present in the moment as you do what you are doing, focused just on what you are doing)
- Receiving bodywork, especially energywork to help you increase your body awareness

SPECIFIC SUGGESTIONS FOR MEDICAL INTUITIVES

- Whole-body breathing.
- Pranayama and other breathing exercises.

- Giving yourself Reiki energy or healing energy in general.
- Use tuning forks over or around your body
- Use floral essential oils or incense (*e.g.*, lavender, frankincense, chamomile, orange, rosemary); stones/crystals (*e.g.*, amethyst, clear quartz, azurite, lapis lazuli); flower essences; or other tools you know about that are centering.

SPECIFIC SUGGESTIONS FOR SPIRIT MEDIUMS

- Breathe with your crown chakra. This technique can help you center yourself and can also be used to make the connection with the spirit realm.
- After you have opened your crown chakra and sense a connection with your spirit helpers, extend your breathing to breathe (subtly) with the energy in the room. Know that your spirit helpers have created a protective circle around the room. Be in this space of being present with the energy of the room, being open and waiting (not looking) for spirits to gather.

Disconnect

Being able to "disconnect" is being able to pull your awareness back into your sense of self without bringing another's stuff with it. It means being able to establish and maintain clear boundaries between you and what you just psychically read (during and after the reading). It might also include clearing the energy within you and/or the room after psychic work. To disconnect, you must be grounded.

GENERAL SUGGESTIONS:

- With your intention, see and/or pull your energy and psychic sense back into your own space. Feel the boundaries around you.
- Get up and shake your hands and let that flow into shaking your whole body.
- Visualize the open door in your third-eye. Now close it with your intention. Also close the top of your head.
- Put your hand on your solar plexus. Affirm, "My energy is with me. Your energy is with you."
- Put your awareness in your feet, and breathe with the energy there. You might also breathe with the center of the Earth to ground yourself.
- Say a brief prayer or affirmation.
- If you placed a cord from your sacrum to the Earth, pull it back into your sacrum.
- Close down your "mind screen" and leave your "psychic room."
- If you are having difficulty disconnecting, try taking off your shoes and walking outside on the ground, take a bath using cleansing essential oils, eat meat, or do what works for you.
- If you want to cleanse the energy in the room (and in you), use one or more of the following:

Smudge with sage or incense.

Light a candle.

Use your intention to fill the room with bright light (green or white)

Ask your spirit helper to release the energy in the room.

Use an affirmation or prayer.

- Take a self-defense class (focused on your physical security). This will carry over to your ability to disconnect psychically.

- Play a music instrument, like a flute, drum, or string instrument, such as an autoharp (lay it on your body/trunk to help you center, as well as to disconnect and clear energy).

- Use tuning forks over or around your body.

- Use cleansing or stimulating essential oils or incense (*e.g.*, peppermint, cypress, lemongrass, tea tree, pennyroyal, sage); stones/crystals (*e.g.*, obsidian, fluorite, smoky quartz, citrine); flower essences; or other tools you know about that are centering.

SPECIFIC SUGGESTIONS FOR SPIRIT MEDIUMS

- Ask your spirit guides to clear the room of any energy that was present during your reading. As you work with your spirit guides, you will build trust in their ability to take care of the energy space when you do spirit communication.

- Visualize the energy leaving the room, as if it is going up a tube into the heavens.

- Set your intention that you own the room, and no one is allowed in your space without your permission. When this is deeply ingrained in you, that you own your space, that alone will clear a room. Practice.

3 Ethics and Boundaries

Your ethics create your boundaries. Good, healthy ethics and boundaries are a necessary part of being psychic for two reasons:

1. You can access the full potential of your psychic sense.
2. You can offer the best psychic insights for yourself and others.

Poor boundaries can lead to being drained physically and emotionally. For professional psychics, this can result in burnout, so they may not be capable of doing this work long term. Also, without good boundaries, your psychic insights could be more about you than what would come through if you were better able to set aside or "boundary" your filter (your perspectives, opinions, and beliefs).

Below are guidelines for you to consider:

1. **Refrain from psychic gossip.** Psychic gossip is using your abilities to gain an advantage over someone else, reading someone just because you want to know something about that person, and telling other people what you pick up psychically about another person.

2. **Refrain from intentionally reading friends, family, and people in your social and work groups.** You will find that you can't help but know things psychically about the people in your lives. But do not intentionally read them. This is about creating healthy boundaries, so that you have healthy relationships. For example, if you told your hairdresser something you got psychically about her, she may feel personally invaded. Even if she appreciates this information, what happens if you pick up something she didn't want you to know? Psychically reading people in your personal life could result in losing relationships.

3. **"When to tell" what you get psychically is an ongoing ethical question.** Of course, there will be times when you get psychic insights about family and friends without even trying. What then? This is always up for your thoughtful consideration of what is ethical. No set guideline works here. You will have to consider the significance of the issue and the people involved and your own integrity and sense

of responsibility. You don't have to tell the person that it came from a psychic source. Before my friends and family knew I was a professional psychic, I would turn what I got psychically into a question or tell them I had a dream about them. It was up to them if they wanted to discuss it. I didn't want to undermine their personal autonomy by suggesting my psychic perspective carried greater weight.

4. **The need to psychically tune into everything in your life may be about your own need to control.** This can result in your crossing boundaries and becoming a controlling, know-it-all person.

5. **Don't set yourself up as the resident psychic in your friendship groups.** This can apply to any group in which you are a member. By setting yourself up as the psychic expert, you no longer have an equal membership status in the group. This can interfere with your developing close friendships, and it diminishes the perspectives, power, and status of other members of the group. This can also lead to your using your ability to gain advantage over others.

6. **Develop healthy psychological and energetic boundaries.** Establishing healthy psychological boundaries carries over in creating healthy boundaries with your psychic abilities. Most of us did not learn how to make healthy boundaries, so it is important to be able to identify when someone violates your boundaries and what to do about it. Know when you violate boundaries as well.

Boundaries—Where You End and I Begin: How to Recognize and Set Healthy Boundaries, 1994, by Anne Katherine

Energetic Boundaries: How to Stay Protected and Connected in Work, Love, and Life, 2011, by Cyndi Dale

7. **Make a commitment to ongoing personal development.** We all need to continue to develop psychologically, intellectually, physically, and spiritually (what lies beyond us, a.k.a. the transpersonal). All of these aspects strengthen the psychic sense and provide a well-grounded, healthy framework for using your psychic abilities. The more you understand yourself and work through relationships and psychological issues, the clearer your psychic sense will be. This will also help keep your ego in check. Intellectual development opens you to new ideas and stimulates curiosity, the bedrock of the psychic sense. Being aware of your body can increase your psychic sense. Improving your physical health will aid you in removing blocks to your psychic abilities. Spiritual development challenges you to expand your ideas about what lays beyond us humans.

8. **Be open to the possibility that what you are getting psychically is wrong or incomplete.** Too much self-doubt about your abilities can weaken the psychic sense. But if you are overconfident about your psychic insights, this too can lead to weakening the psychic sense. Create a balance between healthy skepticism and sufficient confidence to trust yourself and your psychic ability.

ETHICS AND BOUNDARIES FOR MEDICAL INTUITIVES

9. **Do not overlay your beliefs on to your clients.** Your role is to pay attention to what your client's body is communicating. If you hold preconceived ideas for how a body or body's energy is supposed to be, you cannot listen fully. Your role is to get information from your client's body.

10. **Do not diagnose or treat physical or mental illness.** The client's empowerment is diminished if you come from the expert role. Any psychic insights you receive are suggestions that require further investigation. Refer clients to healthcare professionals when appropriate.

11. **Maintain confidentiality.** What transpires during psychic readings, particularly those on someone's health, must be kept between you and that person. If you feel a need to process what came up during a session, do that with an appropriate mentor who also has a commitment to maintain confidentiality.

12. **Be careful about relying too much on spirit guides to live your life.** You are responsible for your life, and spirit communication is not a replacement for developing your own inner resources to live your life effectively. If you need to check with a spirit (or a human person) every time you make a decision, you might want to look deeper within yourself to discover why you have this need.

13. **Set clear boundaries/intention when working with spirits.** Set boundaries with spirits like you would with any person. You are in charge, and you are the one who decides when a spirit is allowed into your space and when the conversation needs to stop.

14. **Angels, ascended masters, divine beings, and other so-called higher level beings do not necessarily have any more access to the "truth" than anyone else (living or not).** I take all information from any spirit, regardless of who they are, as advice. And their opinions may or may not be helpful. Always integrate any psychic or spirit advice with other sources, such as your own analytical skills or counsel from trusted people. Maintain your autonomy when communicating with spirits. It is never wise to make life decisions based solely on a psychic reading or a spirit's advice (or on any one source).

15. **Just like people in our world, spirits may not have your best interests at heart.** If you are feeling negative energy or getting messages that are not in your best interest, this is not from a spirit guide. Professional help for these matters is more readily available today in the form of therapists who respect psychic phenomena, shamans, Wiccan or Pagan practitioners, books, and others in the psychic field. Use the same good judgment about spirits that you would to determine if a person in your life is offering a healthy relationship. Be aware of "red flags" that indicate a spirit is not a healthy energy to communicate with:

    • The spirit says only you can communicate with that spirit.

    • The spirit wants you to spend time with that spirit only.

    • The spirit says negative things about other spirits or your friends and family.

    • The spirit says things or expects you to do things that are against your better judgment and against the advice from trusted friends, family, and advisors.

    • The spirit is critical or harsh.

    • The spirit overly compliments you, like you are better and more special than anyone else because you communicate with this spirit.

    • The spirit's energy feels negative, heavy, dark, and/or dense. (http://paganwiccan.about.com/od/samhainmagic/p/Is-Your-Spirit-Guide-Really-There-To-Help.htm)

If some of the prior occurs with spirit communication, you may not be communicating with a spirit. This could be a projection of your own psychological need for attention. The spirit may feel very real. But our minds can create tangible energy that may seem like a spirit, but isn't. Seek professional help to work on your inner self. You do not have to communicate with, or be around, negative, difficult spirits.

Inner and Energy Boundaries

In my experience, when I create good inner boundaries, my physical and energy bodies are usually strong, too. A separation doesn't actually exist between inner and physical energy boundaries. But it helps to segment them to assure that you have developed strong boundaries to do psychic work. I encourage you to identify the areas of personal growth that you require and seek support for them.

I refer to "inner" boundaries as:

• Knowing yourself and feeling good in your skin

• Creating good emotional health

• Having the abilities and tools to get over yourself and to deal with life

We regularly send an energetic message out into the world about ourselves. This has to do with how you carry yourself. It's the energy message that communicates the above three issues about yourself. It's also what we say and how we act, but perhaps more importantly, it's what our body's energy is saying that people unconsciously "read." You will find it helpful to spend time journaling about:

WHAT ENERGY MESSAGE AM I SENDING OUT INTO THE WORLD ABOUT MYSELF?

It is helpful to consider a variety of models for understanding how body energy functions. You do not have to hold their beliefs to learn from these models. One view is that each of us has an etheric energy body that is connected to the chakras. There are many books and systems of thought about the number, level, and intensity of one or more subtle energy bodies that we have. One such system is that created by Barbara Brennan, a former NASA physicist who developed a detailed anatomy of the auric field. Her school teaches how to "read" these multi-layers and bring healing and harmony to the aura. A healthy aura promotes strong energy boundaries.

Another model for understanding body energy is acupuncture. This ancient health practice views the body as having lines and nodes (or points) of energy throughout the body. When there is trauma to the body, whether it is physical or emotional, the flow of energy is affected. Acupuncture is used to restore this flow through particular meridians. When your energy body is in balance, like that achieved with the assistance of acupuncture, we are better able to maintain good energy boundaries.

Dream researchers and astral projectors explore how the energy or spirit body leaves the physical body. This occurs naturally and mostly without our remembering it during the dream state. But we can also learn to consciously journey out of the body and experience other realms of being. Travelers learn to protect and be in control of their energy body. This is another way to get to know your energy body and develop strong energy boundaries.

Some Earth-based cultures understand the Earth body and human body to have energies that interact with each other. You may have heard of meridians of energy on the Earth as well as nodes or vortexes discussed on television on the History Channel. Some locations that are considered sacred sites around the world are thought to have been built on these sacred vortexes of energy. People have had unusual experiences when visiting these areas. Material on Earth-based spirituality (*e.g.*, pagan, Wiccan, Native American) can provide you with information on how to work with both Earth energies and your own body energy.

There is also a body of work dealing with removing energy cords and attachments. Sometimes referred to as shamanic work, bodyworkers and body-centered psychotherapists brought these concepts into our Western mainstream culture. They offer soul retrievals to assist their clients to put back the parts of themselves that have been lost or taken through trauma. I started getting soul retrievals and cord work done by bodyworkers in the 1980s. But today, soul retrievals aren't so much done to the client by the practitioner, but rather are facilitated and taught to clients, so they can learn how to do this for themselves.

How to Create and Support Healthy Energy Boundaries

Energy boundaries are not just something you do when doing psychic work. It is a way of living, so you don't pick up energy that doesn't belong to you. I call this "psychic lint." Following are some ideas to remove the "lint." Pick the ones that resonate with you.

1. **Increase your body awareness.**
   You need to be body aware to know when your energy boundaries are being violated (and when you are stepping over someone else's boundaries). Incorporate body awareness exercises and techniques into your life on a daily basis.
   When I first got Polarity Therapy (an energy technique) in the early 1980s, I couldn't feel my body. The bodyworker told me about the movement of energy in my body during the session, but I was unable to sense it. After getting additional bodywork and going to massage school, I finally felt energy in and around me. So, it's far easier now for me to create healthy energy boundaries.

2. **Professional Support.**
   At times, we need the assistance of professionals to release stuck or negative energy. Just like a car, we can benefit from an energetic tune-up. A variety of practitioners are available today, including energyworkers, massage therapists, chakra/aura balancers, acupuncturists, holistic psychotherapists, herbalists, and more. Find one or more professionals so you have this support when you need it.

3. **Water.**
   Not only cleansing to your physical body, water clears the energetic body as well. Stand under the shower head, letting the water flow on the top of your head and down your body. Feel any stuff that's in your energy body fall down and into the drain. Occasionally, take a bath with herbs and oils that support the body. Put your feet in a creek. Sit by a waterfall and feel your stuff flow down the falls into a pool of healing energy. You can visualize this, but why not visit a waterfall? Go to the ocean and sit in the sun, feeling the immense waves flow over you and clearing your energy body. Oceans have negative ions that are cleansing and uplifting. Consider putting a water fountain in your home or in your yard—it helps move energy.

4. **Dry Skin Brushing.**
   Use a natural fiber brush with a long handle to brush your body. Always brush towards the heart. This not only clears toxins from your physical body, but it also cleanses the energy body. It can be invigorating as well. (www.whole-body-detox-diet.com/dry-skin-brushing.html)

5. **Self-Massage.**
   Give yourself massage. It is relaxing and can increase your body awareness. Besides it just feels good. Videos are available on-line: www.youtube.com/watch?v=-RTP4GVnqCw

6. **Conversations with Your Body.**
   Increase your body awareness by connecting to a specific part of your body. Breathe with this body area. When you feel a connection, ask what it wants to tell you. Your body has a perspective on life that might be different from that of your analytical mind.

7. **Sense Your Aura.**
   As you go through your day, periodically check your aura. Get a feel for where it ends—where is its boundary? If you do this check when in different life situations, you will notice that your aura boundary is likely different.

8. **Chakra Check.**
   Find a particular chakra that wants to communicate with you about your life. As you go through your day, periodically tune into this chakra. Put your sense of self inside this chakra. Perhaps breathe with it.

Then ask, "What do I need to know?" or "What do you want to tell me?" Experiment with your other chakras.

9. **Close Your Energy Field.**

Play with being invisible. Sense the energy around your body, and then pull it in closer to yourself. Or put on a Harry Potter invisibility cloak. Notice how people relate to you.

10. **Breath Awareness.**

Breath is energy. When you hold your breath, energy doesn't flow. Just pay attention to your breath without criticism. Awareness is important—so don't just do better breathing; be with your breath.

11. **Wood Bowl.**

Get a hand-turned wooden bowl. Place it over a body area—maybe one that you are having problems with. This idea came from my massage therapist, Rosalie Winstead. During a session, she put a bowl on my lower back while she worked on the rest of my back. Soon I felt a trickle of what felt like water flow from my lower back down a leg. It was such a tangible feeling, that it took me aback! Rosalie got this idea from reading about Tibetan monks who ritually washed their hands in wood bowls before meditation—not with water, but with the bowl itself. She thought if this could help them, then why not use a wood bowl with her clients to "wash" the body.

12. **Henna Tattoos.**

Get a friend to design a freehand henna tattoo somewhere on your body, or do it yourself. Put your attention with the drawing as it is being done. Focus on this particular henna tattoo as establishing an energetic boundary for your whole body—that this tattoo is creating a web of protection in your auric field. Henna tattoos disappear over a short period of time. You can usually get materials at health food stores or online.

13. **Sacred Symbols.**

Throughout time, people have used symbols for protection. Use symbols familiar to your background or research ones used in ancient times in other cultures. Draw the symbols, put them around your home, draw them on your body using henna, visualize them, and create other ways to use symbols to create good energy.

14. **Green Space.**

Getting out into Nature helps to ground us and free us from difficulties. Researchers have found that getting kids, particularly those with autism, out into green space often settles them down.

15. **Smudging.**

Light a sage stick and blow out the flame after it gets going. Then fan the smoke over your body (or room) to "clear the air."

16. **Energy Sponge.**

Imagine that you have a sponge in your hands (or use a real one). Dab your body with the sponge. Then hold it in front of your belly button, about one foot from your body. See any tight, tense, difficult, negative energy leave your body and enter into the sponge. It is soaking up this stuff—it's like a magnet taking anything out that isn't serving you. When the cleansing feels complete, squeeze the sponge, seeing all that stuff go into the Earth to be cleared. Or take the actual sponge and rinse it under water, squeezing out all that stuff.

17. **Build a Ball of Energy.**

Slowly wave your arms with palms up in a figure eight, in front of your body like in Tai Chi collecting good energy in the universe to support you. Feel the energy or light forming into a ball of energy. Stop moving your hands, and hold the ball. Thank the universe for this gift. Then take the ball and slowly glide it over your head and down through your body, feeding your body with wonderful energy! If you don't feel a ball of energy, practice.

18. **Medicine Bags.**

Get a special, small bag or make one yourself. Put in items that are special to you, for example, crystals, stones, herbs, symbols, and mementos. Carry the bag with you. It can help you create an energy field of protection.

19. **Sound, Music, Drumming, Crystal Bowls.**

Vibrational healing created by sound can assist you in clearing and maintaining healthy energy boundaries. Try using a drum or autoharp near or on your body—feel the vibrations resonate with your body. Drumming and crystal bowl events may be offered in your community. Chanting is another way to use sound that shifts energy within and around your body and in the room.

20. **Casting a Circle and Calling in the Directions.**

You can learn more about these techniques from material on paganism, Wicca, Shamanism, and other Earth-based spirituality. Call in the directions (east, south, west, north, Heavens, Earth) using drums and rattles pointed at each of the directions. Invite the spirits of these directions to be present with you. Create a circle in your mind or set one up with candles or use a stick to point out the circle being made. An energetic boundary is set up, using both techniques and your intention. This tool is typically used for a specific reason, like for a ritual or ceremony. But you can use this to create a sacred space for meditation or psychic work.

21. **Feng Shui.**

Create a positive, supportive environment in your home and office by using Feng Shui techniques. Lots of books and websites are available today for you to do-it-yourself. This tool is about creating a balance to allow a good flow of supportive energy into your environment.

22. **Wind Chimes.**

First, they have a beautiful sound. And remember from #19 that sound shifts energy. They are also used in Feng Shui. Experiment with low and high-pitched tones.

23. **Sea Salt and Citrus.**

Put sea salt in a container (it may as well be Kosher salt—it's blessed!). Mix lemon rind, juice, and/or lemon oil into the salt. Set the container in a corner of the room or wherever you feel inclined to do so. It will absorb negative energy. Students were having a particularly difficult time once in a classroom where I was teaching. The owner of the store set a cup of this salt in the corner. No one knew about it but me. The room's energy and the students soon settled down.

24. **Cleanliness & Organization.**

Clutter around you can contribute to clutter in your energy field. Which comes first? It doesn't really matter. When you clean your space, you will likely have a clearer mind and energy field. This is all about Feng Shui in that clutter stops energy from flowing and moving. But I know people who use clutter to create boundaries.

25. **Prayer and Contemplation.**

These tools have long been used to release worldly matters, so one can connect to deeper sources of wisdom. You do not have to be an adherent of any particular religious or spiritual approach. Try using a confessional prayer, one where you talk about your part in difficult experiences. Try kneeling at the bedside and use petitionary prayer to ask for help. And be sure to find time to be alone and quiet so you can contemplate the meaning of your life.

The foregoing list of tools is included in the Boundary Checks card on the next page. Photocopy the card and carry it with you daily. The card is also available at the back of this workbook, and it can be easily cut from the book and copied. Check off the items as you do them. You have created healthy energy boundaries when you no longer need the card to remind you to do good boundaries.

Boundary Checks
TUNE IN & CLEAR ENERGY

CHECKS

[ ] Tired?

[ ] Feeling overwhelmed?

[ ] Uncomfortable with this energy?

[ ] Overfeeling others' emotions?

[ ] Overeating?

[ ] Am I feeling a need to overgive?

WAYS TO CLEAR & BOUNDARY

[ ] Wash hands

[ ] Take a bath or shower

[ ] Put hand over solar plexus

[ ] Dry skin brushing

[ ] Self-massage

[ ] Talk with a body area

[ ] Check a chakra; smile

[ ] Close energy field

[ ] Observe my breath

[ ] Put wood bowl on body area

[ ] Draw henna tattoo

[ ] Carry or hang sacred symbol

[ ] Go into green space outside

[ ] Do whole body breathing

[ ] Shake hands...body

[ ] Smudge with sage or incense

[ ] Create/use energy sponge

[ ] Build a ball of energy

[ ] Carry medicine bag

[ ] Drum, chimes, tuning forks around body or room

[ ] Cast circle / call in directions

[ ] Balance room with Feng Shui

[ ] Put sea salt & citrus in room

[ ] Clean & organize room

[ ] Pray & contemplate

[ ] Smile

CHECKS

[ ] Tired?

[ ] Feeling overwhelmed?

[ ] Uncomfortable with this energy?

[ ] Overfeeling others' emotions?

[ ] Overeating?

[ ] Am I feeling a need to overgive?

WAYS TO CLEAR & BOUNDARY

[ ] Wash hands

[ ] Take a bath or shower

[ ] Put hand over solar plexus

[ ] Dry skin brushing

[ ] Self-massage

[ ] Talk with a body area

[ ] Check a chakra; smile

[ ] Close energy field

[ ] Observe my breath

[ ] Put wood bowl on body area

[ ] Draw henna tattoo

[ ] Carry or hang sacred symbol

[ ] Go into green space outside

[ ] Do whole body breathing

[ ] Shake hands...body

[ ] Smudge with sage or incense

[ ] Create/use energy sponge

[ ] Build a ball of energy

[ ] Carry medicine bag

[ ] Drum, chimes, tuning forks around body or room

[ ] Cast circle / call in directions

[ ] Balance room with Feng Shui

[ ] Put sea salt & citrus in room

[ ] Clean & organize room

[ ] Pray & contemplate

[ ] Smile

Boundary Checks

TUNE IN & CLEAR ENERGY

CHECKS

[   ] Tired?

[   ] Feeling overwhelmed?

[   ] Uncomfortable with this energy?

[   ] Overfeeling others' emotions?

[   ] Overeating?

[   ] Am I feeling a need to overgive?

WAYS TO CLEAR & BOUNDARY

[   ] Wash hands

[   ] Take a bath or shower

[   ] Put hand over solar plexus

[   ] Dry skin brushing

[   ] Self-massage

[   ] Talk with a body area

[   ] Check a chakra; smile

[   ] Close energy field

[   ] Observe my breath

[   ] Put wood bowl on body area

[   ] Draw henna tattoo

[   ] Carry or hang sacred symbol

[   ] Go into green space outside

[   ] Do whole body breathing

[   ] Shake hands…body

[   ] Smudge with sage or incense

[   ] Create/use energy sponge

[   ] Build a ball of energy

[   ] Carry medicine bag

[   ] Drum, chimes, tuning forks
around body or room

[   ] Cast circle / call in directions

[   ] Balance room with Feng Shui

[   ] Put sea salt & citrus in room

[   ] Clean & organize room

[   ] Pray & contemplate

[   ] Smile

What Are Your Blocks?

THE FILE BOX

Use this technique to discover blocks you might not already know about or to get added insights into the blocks that you are aware of.

Get in a relaxed space with both your body and mind grounded and centered.

Imagine a loving being is standing next to you. This presence wants the very best for you. The being is holding a file box. Reach inside your head and pull out file folders of outmoded beliefs, life problems, and whatever is blocking your full psychic ability. Put each folder into the box that the loving being is holding. Keep pulling them out as you think about what's getting in your way.

Then ask the loving being to show you a block you don't know about or to help you with one specific block you can't seem to shift. Then reach deep inside your body, and pull out a red file folder. Open the file, and out comes information about what's blocking you. Take a moment to learn about what's in this file. If it's unclear, come back later to this exercise. When you are finished, put the file in the box.

The loving being puts on the lid to the box and tells you, "I'll help you with this now."

Feel relief come over you, and be in this space for as long as you'd like.

4 The Conscious Mind Crutch

You are doing a psychic reading for Sandy. She wants a new job. You start the reading by moving your energy to be with Sandy and her concern about a new job. You wait for something to come to you. Clairvoyance is the first to give you insights. In your mind's eye, you see Sandy sitting in a small boat. There's a fishing rod in the boat. But Sandy hasn't put it in the water.

You are excited that you got something that you are pretty sure is meaningful about Sandy's job dilemma. You tell her what you see. Then you say that she can't change her job situation until she actually tries to do something about it. She wants a new job, but she's not doing anything to get one. Sandy agrees that you are correct.

Since you are new at giving readings, you are thrilled that you got something that made sense to Sandy. The two of you talk about how she could look for a job, what kinds of jobs suit her, and ways to improve her resume. Sandy seems to be engaged and eager to take these steps to get a better job. Both you and Sandy think this was a helpful reading.

The problem is that most of the reading was coming from your conscious, thinking, analytical mind—not from a psychic source. Beginning psychics are often so happy to have gotten something correct, that they spend the next ten minutes or more interpreting what the "clairs" gave them. And they give counseling advice. This leads to superficial readings that seem helpful on the surface, but fail to give the person sufficient information to make more informed decisions.

So, you do the reading differently. You have learned not to interpret the clairvoyant image you get. This time you tell Sandy just what you got psychically—she is sitting in a boat with a fishing rod not in the water. As she is about to say something, you stop her so that what she says doesn't divert you from doing your psychic work. You put your energy back with the image you got. Your presence is with Sandy in the boat. You don't go looking for what this means. Instead you just sit with this image, waiting for your "clairs" to give you more when ready.

After a few moments of patient, non-trying, you psychically see a huge shark circling Sandy's boat. You clairaudiently hear it snarl! You wait again for a fuller understanding to present itself before telling Sandy what you are getting.

Then you know; it just comes immediately to you through claircognizance that Sandy has something going on in her life that is ready to attack her, if she makes a move in any direction to change her life. All the details of her personal life come flowing to you. Present now with the initial clairvoyant image, you are aware that Sandy is crying as you share what you are getting. You stay with the image, giving all you get until it is finished. You are fully in the psychic zone now. All that you are getting is coming from the psychic part of your mind. Your thinking mind nudges a tissue box towards Sandy, and you say something about it being okay to cry. But that's another part of you doing what's appropriate. You are primarily connected with what you are getting psychically, and that image knows you are really listening and so gives you more and more.

Beginning students use their conscious, thinking minds to fill in the gaps of what they get psychically. Don't process psychic insights with your conscious mind by interpreting what you get—that's a crutch. You have to stay with the energy of what you are reading. I have addressed this in previous chapters. It's included again in this chapter on getting unstuck, because it is probably the single-most important issue that can block you from getting the best, most helpful psychic information. Psychics who don't use the conscious mind crutch give full-bodied readings with rich information for their clients. Refer back to pages 38-39 for instructions on how to set aside the Conscious Mind Crutch so it doesn't get in the way of your psychic skills.

The conscious mind crutch can happen for three reasons: 1) You haven't learned how to set aside your thinking mind and value your psychic insights. 2) Going deeper during a reading may trigger your own unresolved, unconscious mind issues, so you might not want to look deeper when reading something—for others and yourself. 3) You don't want to be wrong—which is a part of reason #2.

1. Our society and our schools train us to value the thinking mind, so we defer to it without even knowing that it's not the only way to understand our world. Every time you use your conscious, thinking mind when doing psychic work, you weaken your psychic sense. Learn to stay in your psychic mind by continuing to tune into what you are getting from the psychic part of your mind. Go back into the energy of what you are getting—stay in your psychic sense. And wait; be patient for more to come. It won't come if you go to your conscious mind to analyze it, give coaching advice, or counseling.

    Why didn't all the information come when you first saw Sandy seated in the boat with the fishing rod? Because you are still developing your psychic sense. After strengthening the "clairs" and allowing psychic insights to come to you instead of trying and looking, psychic insights will come faster—as long as you don't use your conscious mind as a crutch. When you are first learning to use your psychic sense, you might not get the full picture with all the details—it doesn't come in a neat box.

    In my experience with students in the Aspen Program, I regularly point out when they are using the conscious Mind Crutch. In the beginning, many don't seem to realize they are not using their psychic sense, but instead their thinking, advice-giving mind. Over the years, some students have joked about how much I nag them about this. But when students come back the following year to coach the current crop of students, they often tell the new students that this one tool made all the difference in the quality and complexity of their readings.

    Don't underestimate the importance of learning this—that your conscious, thinking mind kicks in automatically to bring understanding to something. We were taught that, and it's difficult to unlearn. As you go about your day, be aware of what parts of your mind are engaging in your activities. And when you are doing psychic work, be aware of when your conscious mind is trying to fill in the gaps. With patience, persistence, and self-awareness, you will one day not use a conscious mind crutch. Your psychic mind will be just as strong as your conscious, thinking mind!

2. When I was in massage school, we were regularly told that we could only take a client where we ourselves had been before. What that meant was that if I wasn't aware of my own inner stuff, then I wouldn't want to see when those same issues came up with a client. Or perhaps the only way I would feel comfortable dealing with my issue would be by drawing clients to me who had the same problem, so I could attempt to work out my stuff through another person. But this isn't healthy.

    This is why doing your inner psychological work is so vital to psychic development. You've got to be willing to keep cleaning out that attic in the unconscious mind. I don't want to get too Freudian here, suggesting that the unconscious mind is full of awful stuff. It's not. Your unconscious mind becomes your friend when you are willing to be aware of the things you've stored in the attic.

3. When students begin to develop their psychic abilities, they are often so concerned about being wrong that they take any psychic insight they get, analyze it with their conscious mind, and then give advice. But analyzing or interpreting and giving advice is not psychic. Unless it comes from a psychic source, it is likely coming from your conscious, thinking mind.

    We are human, and sometimes—many times—we are wrong. When we begin to learn anything new, we are often more wrong than right. It seems that when it comes to psychic information, we think we have to be right all the time from the beginning. It will be easier to develop your psychic abilities if you lighten up on yourself and get comfortable with being wrong.

    In my experience teaching psychic classes, I have seen students so focused on getting every detail, every reading, and every psychic game and exercise correct that they get frustrated and blocked. This issue can be so important to some students that I now recommend doing psychic games and exercises in the beginning without checking to see if you are correct. If you care more about exercising the "muscle" than being a perfect psychic, you are more likely to actually develop stronger psychic skills.

    In a sense, being overly concerned with the need to be right may be indicative of low self-esteem. The conscious mind is used to avoid whatever is unresolved and getting in the way of being psychic.

BLOCKS ARE A NORMAL PART OF LIFE!

Heck, blocks are a normal part of life! Who hasn't experienced stage fright, being tongue-tied, sweaty-hands anxiety, and being stumped? These are all blocks we have dealt with at one time or another. It's what former soccer player Sian Beilock talked about on the PBS show *NOVA, How Smart Can We Get* (check www.pbs.org). Sian was a great soccer player and, one day, a national coach came to see her play. She had a chance to get on the Olympic team. Under high pressure to perform, Sian choked and played terribly (a.k.a. she's human). And she didn't get on the Olympic team.

Sian learned from that experience—she moved through being "choked" like you must be willing to move through blocks to be more psychic. Sian explored the phenomenon of being "choked" as a professor in the Department of Psychology at the University of Chicago. She studies the cognitive and neural substrates of learning skills, as well as the mechanisms by which performance breaks down in high-stress or high-pressure situations. Doing a psychic reading for a stranger can be high-stress, high-pressure for students. Here's what she learned in one of her studies to reduce the stress.

Before taking an important math test, some students journaled for fifteen minutes about their test anxiety. Other students just sat there. After the test, the ones who had journaled, did better on the test. Experiment with this the next time you do psychic work. For fifteen minutes, write about how you are feeling about using your psychic abilities. And see what happens.

Check out the book: *Choke: What the Secrets of the Brain Reveal About Getting it Right When You Have To*, 2010, by Sian Beilock.

NOTES

NOTES

NOTES

CHAPTER 6
It's There When You Need It
Using Your Psychic Ability in Everyday Life

Three cards are provided in this chapter that you can copy and carry with you to build your psychic skills. The cards are also available at the back of this workbook, and they can easily be cut from the book and copied. Check off the items as you do them.

You don't have to spend hours to get psychic insights. Spend just five to ten minutes off and on throughout the day using these cards.

1 Daily Psychic Check-ins

Use the card on the **next page** to strengthen your psychic skills. It takes seconds to a few minutes and can be integrated into other things you are doing. Even if you only have limited time and don't get any insights, do some or all of the check-ins every day. This builds the habit, the foundation for your psychic sense. If you have walked in the world for too long dismissing your psychic sense, you need to convince this part of you that you are serious about using this innate ability. (The numbers in parentheses following each entry will direct you to a page in this book for insight into the topic.)

Daily Psychic Check-ins

DO SEVERAL EACH DAY:

[ ] Dreams last night? (30)
[ ] What will today be like? (191)

ANTICIPATE:

[ ] How many emails/texts? (134)
[ ] Who's there (phone/door)? (134)
[ ] Check-in with the energy of where I'm about to go (129, 134)

BE CREATIVE:

[ ] Paint/Draw (126)
[ ] Doodle (127)
[ ] Write poetry or stories (127)
[ ] Dance without rules (127)
[ ] Play an instrument (127)

BODY AWARENESS:

[ ] Clear chakras (103)
[ ] How does my body feel? (20, 61, 117)
[ ] Check aura; smile with a chakra (169)

BREATHING EXERCISES:

[ ] 3rd eye (10)
[ ] Crown chakra (89)
[ ] Brain lobes: occipital, temporal (66, 70)
[ ] Observe my breath (28, 100)
[ ] Whole body breathing (104)
[ ] Extend breath to something pull it back (129-130)

FOCUS ON:

[ ] Feeling (Clairsentience) (56)
[ ] Seeing (Clairvoyance) (64)
[ ] Hearing (Clairaudience) (68)
[ ] I just know! (Claircognizance) (74)
[ ] Smelling (Clairalience) (80)
[ ] Tasting (Clairgustance) (83)

MENTAL FOCUS:

[ ] Time alone (22, 99, 115)
[ ] Enter my psychic room (99)
[ ] Meditate (99-100)
[ ] Journal (100)

NATURE AWARENESS:

[ ] Just be with/breathe with Nature (130)
[ ] Talk with Nature (132)

PLAY OUTSIDE MY RUT:

[ ] Smile (109)
[ ] Hum or make up a song (109)
[ ] Drive different route (110)
[ ] Observe the unobvious (110)
[ ] Use non-dominant hand (110)
[ ] Do cloud busting (111)
[ ] Call someone unexpectedly (111)
[ ] Do an act of random kindness (111)

[ ] **ENTER INTO SLEEP, "AM I PSYCHIC?" (116)**

Daily Psychic Check-ins

DO SEVERAL EACH DAY:

[ ] Dreams last night? (30)
[ ] What will today be like? (191)

ANTICIPATE:

[ ] How many emails/texts? (134)
[ ] Who's there (phone/door)? (134)
[ ] Check-in with the energy of where I'm about to go (129, 134)

BE CREATIVE:

[ ] Paint/Draw (126)
[ ] Doodle (127)
[ ] Write poetry or stories (127)
[ ] Dance without rules (127)
[ ] Play an instrument (127)

BODY AWARENESS:

[ ] Clear chakras (103)
[ ] How does my body feel? (20, 61, 117)
[ ] Check aura; smile with a chakra (169)

BREATHING EXERCISES:

[ ] 3rd eye (10)
[ ] Crown chakra (89)
[ ] Brain lobes: occipital, temporal (66)
[ ] Observe my breath (28, 100)
[ ] Whole body breathing (104)
[ ] Extend breath to something pull it back (129-130)

FOCUS ON:

[ ] Feeling (Clairsentience) (56)
[ ] Seeing (Clairvoyance) (64)
[ ] Hearing (Clairaudience) (68)
[ ] I just know! (Claircognizance) (74)
[ ] Smelling (Clairalience) (80)
[ ] Tasting (Clairgustance) (83)

MENTAL FOCUS:

[ ] Time alone (22, 99, 115)
[ ] Enter my psychic room (99)
[ ] Meditate (99-100)
[ ] Journal (100)

NATURE AWARENESS:

[ ] Just be with/breathe with Nature (130)
[ ] Talk with Nature (132)

PLAY OUTSIDE MY RUT:

[ ] Smile (109)
[ ] Hum or make up a song (109)
[ ] Drive different route (110)
[ ] Observe the unobvious (110)
[ ] Use non-dominant hand (110)
[ ] Do cloud busting (111)
[ ] Call someone unexpectedly (111)
[ ] Do an act of random kindness (111)

[ ] **ENTER INTO SLEEP, "AM I PSYCHIC?" (116)**

2 "Running Your Clairs"

Remind yourself to run through all your "clairs" when seeking psychic insights. Carry the sheet below to remind you to use all the "clairs," including psychic smelling and tasting—often left out when using the psychic sense.

RUNNING YOUR CLAIRS
Use all your "clairs" to get insights to a question.

YOUR QUESTION:

_____
_____
_____
_____
_____
_____

CLAIRSENTIENCE – PSYCHIC FEELING (EMOTIONS & ENERGY)
What do I feel about this?

CLAIRVOYANCE – PSYCHIC SEEING
What do I see about this?

CLAIRAUDIENCE – PSYCHIC HEARING
What do I hear about this?

CLAIRCOGNIZANCE – PSYCHIC KNOWING
What do I know about this?

CLAIRGUSTANCE – PSYCHIC TASTING
Is there a taste associated with this?

CLAIRALIENCE – PSYCHIC SMELLING
Is there a scent or odor associated with this?

YOUR QUESTION:

_____
_____
_____
_____
_____
_____

CLAIRSENTIENCE – PSYCHIC FEELING (EMOTIONS & ENERGY)
What do I feel about this?

CLAIRVOYANCE – PSYCHIC SEEING
What do I see about this?

CLAIRAUDIENCE – PSYCHIC HEARING
What do I hear about this?

CLAIRCOGNIZANCE – PSYCHIC KNOWING
What do I know about this?

CLAIRGUSTANCE – PSYCHIC TASTING
Is there a taste associated with this?

CLAIRALIENCE – PSYCHIC SMELLING
Is there a scent or odor associated with this?

3 A Quick-and-Easy Method to Get Psychic Information

Use the card on the next page to get insights into a question. If you'd like, schedule a specific day of the week for reading questions. Over time, this will program your mind to expect to be particularly psychic on that day.

1. **Get a small notebook to record your insights about your question.**

   If you create a special notebook to be used just for the days you want to get psychic messages, your psychic mind will be triggered in a good way when you carry this particular notebook. Yes, you can use an electronic device—but there is something to how writing is stored in your mind.

2. **Write a clear, concise question.**

   The clearer your question, the clearer you create the energy around it and the easier and more direct the insights will be. This is true whether you are using your own psychic abilities or seeking out a professional psychic for insights.

3. **Journal about how you would answer the question now.**

   Describe what's going on concerning the question. Make a list of pros and cons for each possible answer or write about your thoughts and feelings for possible approaches to the issue. Experiment with including this step and eliminating it from this procedure. For some, this step seeds the energy around the question and helps to prepare for psychic work. For others, this step may keep you stuck in your analytical mind. If the latter happens to you, try eliminating this step, leaving the analytical part of your decision-making for when you have gathered psychic insights.

4. **Choose five or more of the techniques listed on the card to gather psychic insights during one day.**

   Get in that quiet, connected zone first. Blend it in throughout your day, using a different technique each time. Page numbers are included on the card to refer back to information about each technique.

5. **Review your psychic insights.**

   What do you think your psychic sense is trying to communicate? If you'd like additional information, use this procedure for two or three days and then set it aside. Insights often come when we aren't trying, and you could get more insights on the off days.

6. **Make a list of possible steps you could take based on the psychic insights you received.**

   Use the technique on **page 136** to psychically consider your options.

7. **Keep a record of the action you took and the outcome.**

   When you review this over time, you will begin to understand the ways in which your own unique psychic sense is communicating with you. This will also help you decide what techniques work best for you.

Write a clear, concise question.

ANALYZE: HOW WOULD YOU ANSWER NOW?

CHOOSE 5+ TECHNIQUES:

Use the technique & then ask your question

[   ] **1.** Send your energy and breath awareness to your question (62)

[   ] **2.** Breathe with your occipital lobe (67)

[   ] **3.** Breathe with your temporal lobes (73)

[   ] **4.** Access the Akashic Records about your question (77-78)

[   ] **5.** Do automatic writing (79)

[   ] **6.** Allow for a smell to give you insights (83)

[   ] **7.** Allow for a taste to give you insights (86)

[   ] **8.** Visualize a movie screen (101)

[   ] **9.** Ask your body (104)

[   ] **10.** Use psychometry (108)

[   ] **11.** Play outside your rut (112)

[   ] **12.** As you enter into sleep, think about your question (122)

[   ] **13.** Do secondary imagery (128)

[   ] **14.** Ask Nature (132)

[   ] **15.** Use a scrying tool (133)

REVIEW PSYCHIC INSIGHTS.

Make a list of possible answers/steps.

Use Envelope Options technique to assess (136)

Take some kind of action.

CHOOSE 5+ TECHNIQUES:

Use the technique & then ask your question

[   ] **1.** Send your energy and breath awareness to your question (62)

[   ] **2.** Breathe with your occipital lobe (67)

[   ] **3.** Breathe with your temporal lobes (73)

[   ] **4.** Access the Akashic Records about your question (77-78)

[   ] **5.** Do automatic writing (79)

[   ] **6.** Allow for a smell to give you insights (83)

[   ] **7.** Allow for a taste to give you insights (86)

[   ] **8.** Visualize a movie screen (101)

[   ] **9.** Ask your body (104)

[   ] **10.** Use psychometry (108)

[   ] **11.** Play outside your rut (112)

[   ] **12.** As you enter into sleep, think about your question (122)

[   ] **13.** Do secondary imagery (128)

[   ] **14.** Ask Nature (132)

[   ] **15.** Use a scrying tool (133)

REVIEW PSYCHIC INSIGHTS.

Make a list of possible answers/steps.

Use Envelope Options technique to assess (136)

Take some kind of action.

4 Precognition—What's in Your Future?

Precognition (Latin: *praecognitio* or *knowledge beforehand*) refers to psychic perception of the future. Precognition can occur during the dream state and the waking state, employing one or more of the "clairs." For the purposes of this workbook, precognition is a term used when you intentionally read the future, while premonition comes of its own accord.

Premonition (Latin: *praemonere* or *forewarning*) and presentiment typically come without effort, when you are not intentionally looking, coming unexpectedly and quickly. Premonitions can involve perceiving the future primarily through the emotions. They seem to be mostly negative, and that's why people often avoid this aspect of their psychic ability. Worrying is not a premonition.

Precognitions and premonitions raise the issue of fate. My personal view is that I don't believe in fate—the idea that our lives are totally planned and set in stone. In my experience as a psychic, about ten percent of what I get about my clients' future, I feel strongly will happen. Most of the time, I psychically receive options for my clients to consider about their future, and that's where I focus most of the reading.

I view psychic insights as offering additional information so that I can make more informed decisions about my life. I don't use precognition to control my life circumstances, so that I don't have to experience bad or difficult things. Life still happens to me—both good and bad things happen. That's life!

So, I recommend that you develop and use your precognitive abilities to assist you with your life—but not to run away from the uncertainties of life by thinking you will have control over them. Otherwise, you may very well miss the richness and joy of living, and perhaps more importantly, the surprising serendipities.

Exercise to Increase Precognitive Skills:

FOLLOW THE UPS AND DOWNS OF A STOCK.

Pick a stock that has a high volume of trading each day, like Apple Computers or General Electric. Each day, tune into the stock, and ask how the stock will close at the end of the day. You could use the same notations the market uses to show how a stock closes: the color "green" for the stock closing up and "red" for closing down. Or you can select an icon that represents the stock, like apple for Apple Computers or a light bulb for General Electric. If you see the apple with a huge bite taken out of it, this could indicate the stock will take a big dive downward. If you see the apple get bigger, the stock goes up. Whatever happens to the apple when you ask it how the computer company's stock will fare that day, just ask the apple what it means. For example, ask what the big bite means.

At first, don't check to see how you did each day. Focus on developing your precognitive abilities instead of whether you are right or wrong. Follow the stock daily for two or more weeks until you get in the rhythm of reading the stock and feel a connection with it. Then read the stock for another week and check how you did on the many financial websites available (www.money.msn.com).

Recap: Will the stock for the computer company, Apple, Inc. (AAPL) be up or down at the close of the trading day? Visualize an apple and then psychically look at it at the end of the trading day—is the apple smaller or larger or just about the same? When you get an answer from the apple, ask it what it means. Record what you get below.

_____

_____

_____

_____

_____

_____

Traffic Light Precognition:

A TOOL FOR READING THE FUTURE

1. Get a blank calendar with the entire year on one page. (An extra calendar can be found on page 195)

2. Write your name and the date at the top of the page.

3. Write the topic of your reading at the top of the page. (Examples: Job/Finances, Relationships, Life Direction.)

4. Hold your name and the topic in your psychic energy awareness. Take a moment to be present with the topic for yourself.

5. Stare at the first month you are reading. Relax your eyes; let them glaze over.
    Expect one of the colors of a traffic light to appear on the month that will be about the topic you are reading. Let one or more colors just pop on to the calendar. It's okay to "see" the color(s) in your mind's eye.

HOLD THE INTENTION THAT:

RED MEANS STOP! DON'T GO FURTHER – THERE IS A PROBLEM.

YELLOW MEANS CAUTION – YOU NEED TO MAKE CHANGES.

GREEN MEANS GO – EVERYTHING IS GOING FINE!

6. Write the color or colors on the paper near the month.

7. Return your psychic awareness and be with the color(s) on the month. Ask the color for specific information that will assist you with your life. Record what you get.

8. Resist interpreting what you get—that's your conscious mind, and it gets in the way of strengthening your psychic sense. No advice giving or counseling—just be psychic!

9. Read the next month (and continue with the remaining months), holding you and the topic of the reading [Job/Finances, Relationships, or Life Direction] in your awareness.

10. When you feel the reading is complete, pull your energy back and look at the entire year. Psychically ask if there is anything else you need to know. Record what you get. Continue with the remaining topics, using a separate calendar to record.

Calendar Precognition
A TOOL FOR READING THE FUTURE

This technique draws upon three "clairs" to use in reading the future. Although the "clairs" are somewhat separated in the methods below, feel free to use two or more "clairs" together.

Calendar precognition can be used to look into your own future, that of a client, or for community and world happenings. I prefer to use a paper calendar with blocks for each day that isn't too visually busy. Free calendars are available on the Internet; try www.printfree.com, or you can make one yourself. You will also find it helpful to develop the skills to visualize a calendar in your mind, especially if you plan to do readings professionally. To build your precognitive skills, get in the habit of reading the week ahead each Sunday.

Use the calendar on the next page to experiment with these techniques.

1. **Clairsentience.**
Move your fingertips slowly over each day to receive physical sensations about the day. Record the physical sensations on the calendar. Interpret what you get after you are finished with the reading. After using this technique for a while, you will likely develop a general code for the significance or meaning of particular physical characteristics. This is a good starting point, but ask questions to get deeper insights.

2. **Clairvoyance and clairaudience.**
Use the paper calendar as a "scrying" tool by staring at a particular day/week/month while allowing your eyes to go out of focus. Let images, thoughts, and words come towards you. Record this on the calendar. Interpret what you get after you are finished with the reading.

3. **Select a polarity of opposites to read the future.**
Gaze at the calendar (paper or in your mind's eye), and ask a question about the future such as, "How will my job be next year?" Expect your psychic sense to give you an answer using one of the polarities below. Be sure to ask for additional insights into whatever you get.

These polarities are clairvoyance:
- Light/Dark
- Red/Yellow/Green (traffic light)
- Happy Face/Neutral Face/Sad Face (if you get an emotion, this is also clairsentience)

These polarities are clairsentient:
- Heat/Cold
- Light/Heavy
- Smooth/Rough

Exercise to Do a Precognitive Reading:

Pair up or do this for yourself. Use one of the calendar precognition techniques to read your partner's, or your, future for the next year. Share additional information you get beyond these questions:

In what months will good things happen?

What months might be difficult?

Let your partner ask something about an area of life in the future (or you select an area of your life for reading yourself): for example: job, finances, relationships. Use Calendar Precognition to give your partner insights.

YEAR:

january	february	march

april	may	june

july	august	september

october	november	december

Exercise to Do a World Precognitive Reading:

Use one of the calendar precognition techniques to read world matters. Hold in your mind the expectation that you will see significant events occurring anywhere in the world in the coming year.

YEAR:

january	february	march

april	may	june

july	august	september

october	november	december

NAME: ....

DATE: ....

YEAR:

january	february	march

april	may	june

july	august	september

october	november	december

NOTES

NOTES

CHAPTER 7

Your Next Step
The Final Frontier is Not Space

(Sorry, Star Trek*)*

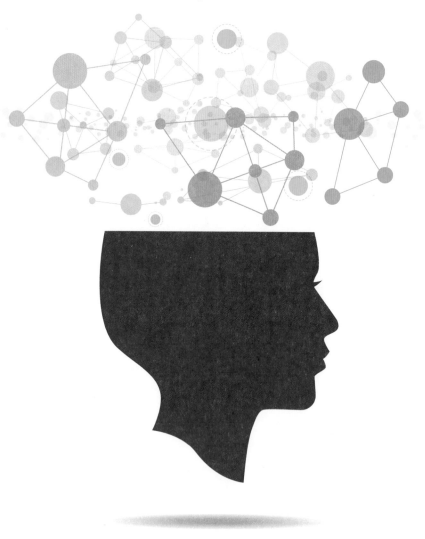

> Space: the final frontier. These are the voyages of the Starship Enterprise.
> Its five-year mission: to explore strange new worlds, to seek out new life and
> new civilizations, to boldly go where no man has gone before.
>
> —Opening to *Star Trek* television show

I flipped on the television one day and happened to see an old commercial with Miss Cleo promoting a psychic phone line. When the commercial ended, the news anchor asked an "expert" whether psychic ability existed. "I don't recall what field the expert was in, but I think he was a psychologist. He replied by saying that the idea that someone could be psychic is magical thinking.

Psychics are often the subject of skeptics. Unfortunately, many skeptics lack the intellectual curiosity necessary to be intelligently skeptical. The debunking of psychic claims often arises out of an individual's belief system, rather than any specific intellectual inquiry or personal experience the skeptic may have had. Psychic abilities are present in people in differing degrees, and some individuals seem to develop their abilities more readily than others. It may be that those who debunk things psychic simply have the least inherent or developed abilities. If they are sufficiently curious, I think debunkers can improve their psychic skills to some extent. The problem with debunkers and others who haven't adequately investigated the psychic sense, or haven't been educated to develop it, is they fuel a belief in our culture that things psychic are silly. But well-known, credible people claim to use this sense.

I was in the last semester of my undergraduate degree in business at George Mason University. One day, the professor told the class that you have now learned how to use all kinds of methods for collecting data to make good business decisions. And someday, you will have experience that you can rely on as well. But sometimes you have to set that aside, and go with your gut instinct—even when it goes against the data and your experience. I knew what that meant. He may have been more comfortable using the term "gut instinct," but that's the same as intuition and the psychic sense.

Larry Dossey, MD, was speaking on miracle cures at the 2008 annual Harvard conference, "Update in Internal Medicine." The physicians were eager to talk about their experiences with spontaneous healing. Then Dr. Dossey brought up the subject of his next book, *Premonitions*. It led to a dynamic discussion—not one that closed off thinking about things psychic. One physician told Dr. Dossey that she knew her patient's test outcomes before she ordered them and got the results. "The times, they are a-changing." And you are a part of that!

Colin Powell, former Secretary of State and US Army general, explained in his book *My American Journey*, "Dig up all the information you can, then go with your instincts. We all have a certain intuition, and the older we get, the more we trust it…I use my intellect to inform my instinct. Then I use my instinct to test all this data." When mainstream people like Dr. Dossey and Secretary Colin Powell celebrate this, they create a comfort zone for all us of us to embrace our psychic abilities. That's when we will finally include psychic training in all levels of our educational system.

I took many college classes that taught me how to collect and analyze business data. In addition to using their rational thinking, scientists, physicians, business professionals, and my professor all viewed input from the psychic sense as a vital part of success. But why isn't it being taught at all levels of education? Psychic ability is a learned skill. It's time to learn how to use it more effectively. We naturally use it anyway, so why not improve this skill?

Those of you who are developing the psychic sense are on the forefront of changing how the psychic sense is viewed in our society. You are joining a long history of well-known and, yes, intelligent people who have claimed to use their psychic abilities in everyday life. Whether they called it intuition, gut instinct, or, as Conrad Hilton called it, "Connie's hunches," they all used their own psychic sense in financial markets, scientific inquiry, and invention. There is already a change afoot that is embracing the psychic sense.

Space is NOT the final frontier. The final frontier is consciousness. Exploring consciousness is an extra-sensory experience that takes us beyond our being. It's not a thing like exploring space with our five senses. It's about transcending the personal, the tangible, and what we already know. Maybe we won't find "life" in the universe until we also explore it with our extra-sensory perception, our psychic sense.

I encourage you to use your critical thinking skills to continue exploring your psychic sense. That's what skeptics do. They are like inquiring scientists—always searching and exploring a subject matter, excited to broaden their understanding, continually open to the possibilities of going beyond what they know at the moment, knowing that nothing can be totally known; but perhaps in the exploration, they might discover something helpful about our world.

Always stay curious. Curiosity is the key to a strong, healthy psychic sense because if you already think you know everything, your mind is closed. For example, if you already have an opinion about spirits and how the afterlife functions and you let that get in the way of a spirit medium reading, your psychic mind is closed. If you hold on to a belief system and overlay that on to your readings, your psychic mind is closed. That's operating from the conscious, thinking mind and maybe the ego-need self as well.

Don't lock up your psychic awareness into a rigidly held dogma box. Think what you will be missing. Set aside your opinions and your world view, so you can allow something different to come to you—psychic insights. Innovation comes when people are willing to step out of the generally accepted boxes of understanding. Our psychic sense gives us the opportunity to set aside what we know to consider the vastness of what we don't know. And what a wonderful journey that can be! It's the space of invention, innovation, and creative imagination. The psychic sense is a part of that final frontier of consciousness, and it's about accessing the full capacities of our minds. Enjoy the journey of exploring your psychic mind!

Be curious, think critically, and have a healthy skepticism!

**"WE MUST CONTINUALLY CHANGE TO BECOME OURSELVES."
—TEILHARD DE CHARDIN**

Index

Daily Psychic Check-ins DO SEVERAL EACH DAY

[　] Dreams last night? (30)

[　] What will today be like? (191)

ANTICIPATE:

[　] How many emails/texts? (134)

[　] Who's there (phone/door)? (134)

[　] Check-in with the energy of where I'm about to go (129, 134)

BE CREATIVE:

[　] Paint/Draw (126)

[　] Doodle (127)

[　] Write poetry or stories (127)

[　] Dance without rules (127)

[　] Play an instrument (127)

BODY AWARENESS:

[　] Clear chakras (103)

[　] How does my body feel? (20, 61, 117)

[　] Check aura; smile with a chakra (169)

BREATHING EXERCISES:

[　] 3rd eye (10)

[　] Crown chakra (89)

[　] Brain lobes: occipital, temporal (66, 70)

[　] Observe my breath (28, 100)

[　] Whole body breathing (104)

[　] Extend breath to something pull it back (129-130)

FOCUS ON:

[　] Feeling (Clairsentience) (56)

[　] Seeing (Clairvoyance) (64)

[　] Hearing (Clairaudience) (68)

[　] I just know! (Claircognizance) (74)

[　] Smelling (Clairalience) (80)

[　] Tasting (Clairgustance) (83)

MENTAL FOCUS:

[　] Time alone (22, 99, 115)

[　] Enter my psychic room (99)

[　] Meditate (99-100)

[　] Journal (100)

NATURE AWARENESS:

[　] Just be with/breathe with Nature (130)

[　] Talk with Nature (132)

PLAY OUTSIDE MY RUT:

[　] Smile (109)

[　] Hum or make up a song (109)

[　] Drive different route (110)

[　] Observe the unobvious (110)

[　] Use non-dominant hand (110)

[　] Do cloud busting (111)

[　] Call someone unexpectedly (111)

[　] Do an act of random kindness (111)

[　] **ENTER INTO SLEEP, "AM I PSYCHIC?" (116)**

Daily Psychic Check-ins DO SEVERAL EACH DAY

[　] Dreams last night? (30)

[　] What will today be like? (191)

ANTICIPATE:

[　] How many emails/texts? (134)

[　] Who's there (phone/door)? (134)

[　] Check-in with the energy of where I'm about to go (129, 134)

BE CREATIVE:

[　] Paint/Draw (126)

[　] Doodle (127)

[　] Write poetry or stories (127)

[　] Dance without rules (127)

[　] Play an instrument (127)

BODY AWARENESS:

[　] Clear chakras (103)

[　] How does my body feel? (20, 61, 117)

[　] Check aura; smile with a chakra (169)

BREATHING EXERCISES:

[　] 3rd eye (10)

[　] Crown chakra (89)

[　] Brain lobes: occipital, temporal (66, 70)

[　] Observe my breath (28, 100)

[　] Whole body breathing (104)

[　] Extend breath to something pull it back (129-130)

FOCUS ON:

[　] Feeling (Clairsentience) (56)

[　] Seeing (Clairvoyance) (64)

[　] Hearing (Clairaudience) (68)

[　] I just know! (Claircognizance) (74)

[　] Smelling (Clairalience) (80)

[　] Tasting (Clairgustance) (83)

MENTAL FOCUS:

[　] Time alone (22, 99, 115)

[　] Enter my psychic room (99)

[　] Meditate (99-100)

[　] Journal (100)

NATURE AWARENESS:

[　] Just be with/breathe with Nature (130)

[　] Talk with Nature (132)

PLAY OUTSIDE MY RUT:

[　] Smile (109)

[　] Hum or make up a song (109)

[　] Drive different route (110)

[　] Observe the unobvious (110)

[　] Use non-dominant hand (110)

[　] Do cloud busting (111)

[　] Call someone unexpectedly (111)

[　] Do an act of random kindness (111)

[　] **ENTER INTO SLEEP, "AM I PSYCHIC?" (116)**

Boundary Checks

TUNE IN & CLEAR ENERGY

CHECKS

[ ] Tired?

[ ] Feeling overwhelmed?

[ ] Uncomfortable with this energy?

[ ] Over feeling others' emotions?

[ ] Overeating?

[ ] Am I feeling a need to over give?

WAYS TO CLEAR & BOUNDARY

[ ] Wash hands

[ ] Take a bath or shower

[ ] Put hand over solar plexus

[ ] Dry skin brushing

[ ] Self-massage

[ ] Talk with a body area

[ ] Check a chakra; smile

[ ] Close energy field

[ ] Observe my breath

[ ] Put wood bowl on body area

[ ] Draw henna tattoo

[ ] Carry or hang sacred symbol

[ ] Go into green space outside

[ ] Do whole body breathing

[ ] Shake hands….body

[ ] Smudge with sage or incense

[ ] Create/use energy sponge

[ ] Build a ball of energy

[ ] Carry medicine bag

[ ] Drum, chimes, tuning forks
     around body or room

[ ] Cast circle / Call in directions

[ ] Balance room with Feng Shui

[ ] Put sea salt & citrus in room

[ ] Clean & organize room

[ ] Pray & contemplate

[ ] Smile

Boundary Checks

TUNE IN & CLEAR ENERGY

CHECKS

[ ] Tired?

[ ] Feeling overwhelmed?

[ ] Uncomfortable with this energy?

[ ] Over feeling others' emotions?

[ ] Overeating?

[ ] Am I feeling a need to over give?

WAYS TO CLEAR & BOUNDARY

[ ] Wash hands

[ ] Take a bath or shower

[ ] Put hand over solar plexus

[ ] Dry skin brushing

[ ] Self-massage

[ ] Talk with a body area

[ ] Check a chakra; smile

[ ] Close energy field

[ ] Observe my breath

[ ] Put wood bowl on body area

[ ] Draw henna tattoo

[ ] Carry or hang sacred symbol

[ ] Go into green space outside

[ ] Do whole body breathing

[ ] Shake hands….body

[ ] Smudge with sage or incense

[ ] Create/use energy sponge

[ ] Build a ball of energy

[ ] Carry medicine bag

[ ] Drum, chimes, tuning forks
     around body or room

[ ] Cast circle / Call in directions

[ ] Balance room with Feng Shui

[ ] Put sea salt & citrus in room

[ ] Clean & organize room

[ ] Pray & contemplate

[ ] Smile

**USE ALL YOUR "CLAIRS" TO GET
INSIGHTS TO A QUESTION.**

YOUR QUESTION:

_____
_____
_____
_____
_____
_____
_____

**CLAIRSENTIENCE – PSYCHIC FEELING
(EMOTIONS & ENERGY)**
What do I feel about this?

CLAIRVOYANCE – PSYCHIC SEEING
What do I see about this?

CLAIRAUDIENCE – PSYCHIC HEARING
What do I hear about this?

**CLAIRCOGNIZANCE – PSYCHIC
KNOWING**
What do I know about this?

CLAIRGUSTANCE – PSYCHIC TASTING
Is there a taste associated with this?

CLAIRALIENCE – PSYCHIC SMELLING
Is there a scent or odor associated with this?

**USE ALL YOUR "CLAIRS" TO GET
INSIGHTS TO A QUESTION.**

YOUR QUESTION:

_____
_____
_____
_____
_____
_____
_____

**CLAIRSENTIENCE – PSYCHIC FEELING
(EMOTIONS & ENERGY)**
What do I feel about this?

CLAIRVOYANCE – PSYCHIC SEEING
What do I see about this?

CLAIRAUDIENCE – PSYCHIC HEARING
What do I hear about this?

**CLAIRCOGNIZANCE – PSYCHIC
KNOWING**
What do I know about this?

CLAIRGUSTANCE – PSYCHIC TASTING
Is there a taste associated with this?

CLAIRALIENCE – PSYCHIC SMELLING
Is there a scent or odor associated with this?

Write a clear, concise question.

ANALYZE: HOW WOULD YOU ANSWER NOW?

CHOOSE 5+ TECHNIQUES:

Use the technique & then ask your question

[ ] **1.** Send your energy and breath awareness to your question (62)

[ ] **2.** Breathe with your occipital lobe (67)

[ ] **3.** Breathe with your temporal lobes (73)

[ ] **4.** Access the Akashic Records about your question (77-78)

[ ] **5.** Do automatic writing (79)

[ ] **6.** Allow for a smell to give you insights (83)

[ ] **7.** Allow for a taste to give you insights (86)

[ ] **8.** Visualize a movie screen (101)

[ ] **9.** Ask your body (104)

[ ] **10.** Use psychometry (108)

[ ] **11.** Play outside your rut (112)

[ ] **12.** As you enter into sleep, think about your question (122)

[ ] **13.** Do secondary imagery (128)

[ ] **14.** Ask Nature (132)

[ ] **15.** Use a scrying tool (133)

REVIEW PSYCHIC INSIGHTS.

Make a list of possible answers/steps.

Use Envelope Options technique to assess (136)

Take some kind of action.

Write a clear, concise question.

ANALYZE: HOW WOULD YOU ANSWER NOW?

CHOOSE 5+ TECHNIQUES:

Use the technique & then ask your question

[ ] **1.** Send your energy and breath awareness to your question (62)

[ ] **2.** Breathe with your occipital lobe (67)

[ ] **3.** Breathe with your temporal lobes (73)

[ ] **4.** Access the Akashic Records about your question (77-78)

[ ] **5.** Do automatic writing (79)

[ ] **6.** Allow for a smell to give you insights (83)

[ ] **7.** Allow for a taste to give you insights (86)

[ ] **8.** Visualize a movie screen (101)

[ ] **9.** Ask your body (104)

[ ] **10.** Use psychometry (108)

[ ] **11.** Play outside your rut (112)

[ ] **12.** As you enter into sleep, think about your question (122)

[ ] **13.** Do secondary imagery (128)

[ ] **14.** Ask Nature (132)

[ ] **15.** Use a scrying tool (133)

REVIEW PSYCHIC INSIGHTS.

Make a list of possible answers/steps.

Use Envelope Options technique to assess (136)

Take some kind of action.